Hardy C. Powers:
Bridge Builder

by
Jerald D. Johnson

Nazarene Publishing House
Kansas City, Missouri

ISBN: 083-411-0733

Printed in
United States of America

10   9   8   7   6   5   4   3   2   1

Hardy C. Powers:
Bridge Builder

Contents

Dedication ·

To my loving wife,
ALICE,
who gave great encouragement to this
project because of the fond memories
she shares with me of wonderful times
enjoyed with our friend
Dr. Hardy C. Powers.

Foreword

It is part of my responsibility and pleasure to read a lot of manuscripts. If I am acquainted with the author or if the subject involves someone I know, I try to psych myself up to be objective.

I did this when starting to read **Hardy C. Powers: Bridge Builder.** As I avidly read the manuscript, however, I found myself becoming subjective through identifying with all the interesting events of this great leader's life.

Those who knew Dr. Powers will be filled with nostalgic memories as the varying circumstances of his life unfold. The author has portrayed this man as a warm, understanding person, yet one who could be firm in his responsibility as a general superintendent in deciding what was best for the church and the kingdom of God.

Everyone will enjoy this book as it gives insight into the leadership of our church and how strong personalities were meshed together in the common cause of advancing scriptural holiness.

—M. A. (BUD) LUNN, *Manager*
Nazarene Publishing House

1

General
Superintendent

The year was 1944, and the Church of the Nazarene faced a crisis which could affect the entire denomination. Because the church was only 36 years into its existence following the 1908 Pilot Point merger, the severity of the crisis threatened the future of the young organization's continued ministry. It was a solemn group of delegates that gathered for the Eleventh General Assembly in the Municipal Auditorium in Minneapolis.

Travel restrictions relating to World War II limited the attendance at this assembly. This served, however, to underscore the determined effort on the part of the delegation to be present to help resolve their problem. Since 1940 the rippling effects of trouble had spread throughout the church. The ever-present rumors had complicated matters greatly, and everywhere people were divided on the issue.

If ever there was a time when the church had needed a united leadership, it was during these crucial war years. Mission work was being threatened in far-off places because of the global conflict. Nazarenes found themselves on opposite sides as national identities were being threatened. In the United States church attendance was sagging due to the demands of the war plants.

The elected denominational leaders given the awesome assignment of being general superintendents had not been able to solve the problem. Not only could they not agree on a solution, but the entire matter centered around one of the general superintendents himself.

General Superintendent Orval J. Nease was the focal point of the church crisis. A matter implying the need for discipline to be applied to a member of this superintendent's family was the specific issue. It had become a particularly sensitive thing for the general superintendent to deal with, and because he had not been as decisive as many felt he should be, a division resulted which would now be distinctly exposed at the General Assembly. The situation had been enlarged and twisted by misunderstandings and miscommunications.

The four incumbent general superintendents—R. T. Williams, J. B. Chapman, H. V. Miller, and Orval J. Nease—were viewed as a board, officially. In reality, their individual leadership styles did not bring them together as such. They were simply four leaders, each endowed with unique administrative skills, leading the church. However, the issue at hand had brought three of them together in a united decision. They relayed this consensus to the fourth, Dr. Nease—in effect, a demand that he resign as general superintendent. When he refused to do so they then agreed that if their colleague was reelected, they would all three resign themselves. It is difficult to imagine what would have happened had their decision been implemented.

From the beginning of the business sessions until the ballot was spread for the incumbents, tensions were mounting. The final tallies were ominous, even for the three somewhat united generals. Dr. Chapman received approval of 91 percent of the delegates for continued leadership as a general superintendent. H. V. Miller was reaffirmed, however, with only 77 percent of the delegates approving his continuing in this capacity. Even the perennially popular R. T. Williams received only an 84 percent mandate to return to office.

The possible crisis of three resigning at once was avoided when the tellers reported that Orval Nease had received only 39 percent of the vote. Two-thirds (66⅔ percent) would be necessary for reelection. Dr. Nease made his way to the podium to give a response to this decision. All knew that what he would have to say would have a direct bearing on the continued proceedings of the assembly.

The denomination was left a meaningful and blessed legacy that day by the reply Dr. Nease gave. "The Church of the Nazarene of which I am a part," he said, "can make it without me. But I cannot make it without the Church of the Nazarene." It was the beginning of a healing process which climaxed with his election to the general superintendency again four years later.

Tensions were broken, and a search began for leadership to replace the one who had not been reelected. An open ballot was distributed, and delegates were instructed to write down any name they chose. Friends of Dr. Nease would continue to support him, although the number would never gain enough strength to swing the election back to him. On that first ballot Hardy C. Powers, the young and relatively unknown district superintendent from Iowa, received a number of votes. It was hardly a decisive expression, however. The dynamic president of Eastern Nazarene College, G. B. Williamson, appeared to be the early favorite for the position. He received 126 votes. Hardy Powers received 62.

A second ballot was cast. This time Williamson received 211 votes and Powers only 52. The trend was obvious, and Williamson's election appeared to be imminent. The third ballot appeared to confirm this assumption. Williamson had 286 votes and Powers had 39.

Dr. Nease had garnered enough votes during the spreading of the first three ballots to block anyone else from receiving the necessary two-thirds. He took the podium again, thanking his friends for their expressions of confidence but urging the delegation to "look in another direction." His support shifted to different persons, and Hardy Powers received a portion of it. This resulted in his vote going up from 39 to 81. But G. B. Williamson's total ran on up to 298, nearly enough to elect him.

However, just prior to the reading of the report on the fourth ballot a recess was declared. The designated purpose of the recess was for the assembly to divide into caucus groups to nominate members to the General Board. Apparently the recess gave opportunity for lively discussion in the hallways of that Municipal Auditorium, for when the General Assembly reconvened, the balloting took a sudden turn in another direction.

After hearing the report on the fourth ballot, the fifth was spread. G. B. Williamson, who had been within 50 votes of being elected, now dropped from 298 to 289 and Hardy Powers' total went from 81 to 247.

On ballot number 6 the assembly was surprised to learn that Powers had surged ahead with 256 votes, and Williamson had dropped back to 245. The seventh ballot was nearly decisive for Powers as he lacked only 14 of the needed number for election. On the eighth ballot Hardy C. Powers was elected the 12th general superintendent of the Church of the Nazarene.

G. B. Williamson was relieved. He had expressed to friends and family that he sincerely felt his time to assume this major position of leadership had not yet come. Furthermore, he felt Hardy Powers was the man the church needed in this hour of crisis.

The announcement of Powers' election was a moment of happy hilarity for the assembled body. The pressure was relieved. The young church had faced and solved its problem and there was occasion for rejoicing.

A native North American Indian delegate found expression for his joy over the decision. He jumped up from where he was sitting and, in full view of many around him, ran over to where Dr. Powers was sitting. He knelt down and began polishing the new general superintendent's shoes. While it was a gesture of humor and goodwill, it was not without its prophetic significance. Time would prove this newly elected church leader to be a special friend of minorities in the United States as well as of non-Americans the world over by important directions in which he would eventually steer his denomination.

The seesaw voting which had taken place between two great men, G. B. Williamson and Hardy C. Powers, would have prophetic overtones as well. Little did they then know how often they would find themselves dueling with each other philosophically on church-related matters the rest of their lives. It must be pointed out here, however, that in spite of interesting differences which would find vocal expression between them, never did such erode their friendship for each other.

The shoe-polishing episode was followed by another bit of drama. I. C. Mathis, a ministerial colleague and special personal friend of Hardy Powers, now left his delegation and crossed over to where the newly elected general was seated. He assumed the role of personally escorting his friend to the platform. The crowd was on its feet, waiting for a word from their newly elected general superintendent.

The response was brief and to the point. The church would have to accustom itself to the leadership style of this man who refused to be pressured into giving quick answers of any kind at any time. First he would have to wait upon the Lord to "think and pray."

"I am sure that I would be either more or less than human if I did not appreciate this expression of your confidence," he said. "But I am not prepared to reply . . . "

Then he continued with his testimony, "I have had just one call since the Monday afternoon when God sanctified me wholly. It was to do His will. I still feel that way . . . and I will continue . . . to seek to know His will. I thank you."

The proceedings had lasted into the evening. He and Mrs. Powers finally were able to be alone in their hotel room to talk to God together about the happenings of the day. Receiving assurance in their hearts that this was indeed God's will for them and for the church, the next day he gave this response as follows:

About six or eight months ago we went one evening, Mrs. Powers and myself, down to the Rock Island station in our city and bid our oldest son good-bye. He was going away to the camp and service of the country, as many other young men have done. As I turned away from that troop train, the ground over which I walked was no longer common ground. I remembered bits of history that I had learned. This incident had brought home to me the fact that our freedom had been purchased at the price of blood; I then said to myself, "How can I live worthily since the privileges that are mine now have been purchased at such fearful cost?"

Back in 1922, in the city of Alhambra, Calif., I attended the first revival campaign that it was ever my privilege to attend in the Church of the Nazarene. Brother Fred Suffield was the evangelist. My heart was touched, and I sought and found a Savior. Some years later in my first pastorate I was reading Dr. Hills' *Holiness and Power* in my room alone. Earnestly before God I let His Word search my heart. There was born within me such an intense hunger that I went to my own altar and sought this experience that we believe and preach and live for. At four o'clock on Monday afternoon God for Christ's sake sanctified me wholly in a very real way. After I came into the Church of the Nazarene, serving in a number of pastorates across the country, everywhere that I went I discovered that others had been before me and had purchased the privileges that I enjoyed at the price of blood. When I was elected to the superintendency of the Iowa District, it was not long before I was in a little church that bore the name in a stained-glass window of Dr. P. F. Bresee. Over that whole state I have traveled, and I have said I am living and enjoying the privileges of membership and fellowship at the cost of blood.

As I stand here on this platform this afternoon, that is the thought that has been gripping my heart and mind. I know the men who have preceded me at this microphone have led us safe thus far, humanly speaking, and I know they have put blood into the Church of the Nazarene. Not only they, but also those who have gone before them. Some time ago I was out on the wind-swept plains of South Dakota, and I made my way out to a little cemetery on the hill and found the grave that bore the name of J. G.

Morrison. We kneeled in the wind with uncovered head and prayed God to help us not to live unworthily of those who have given us their life and blood for our church today. There are times when the sense of responsibility to God and those who have gone before us is so great as to be oppressive.

I appreciate your expression of confidence, and I am accepting the responsibility with all it means with the full expectation of contributing my all and doing my best. As I walk along this pathway, I shall endeavor to remember first it has been stained with the blood of Him who purchased our salvation and then with the blood of many mighty men. As I take up this responsibility and accept the obligation as mine, I shall need much patience from you and a generous portion of your prayers. But I pledge you this as we face the future: that I shall seek to live worthily so that when life is through, I shall have no regrets and be unembarrassed in the atmosphere of heaven. Thank you for your expression of confidence in the vote of last evening.

Present in that assembly was former General Superintendent Dr. J. W. Goodwin. He had been elected to this office in 1916 and had served until 1940, at which time he was made general superintendent emeritus. His presence was significant, for he was, as it were, a strong link to the past. What he would have to say concerning this particular General Assembly would carry a lot of weight and help determine its place in the young denomination's history. He was called upon to respond to Dr. Powers' remarks. His comments served to help unite the entire church and became one of his own last and most significant expressions of leadership. He spoke as follows:

A man who seeks a place of responsibility is a fool. And I believe that while that is a strenuous statement, there is very much truth in it. I know something of the care and something of the burden that is thrust upon a man when he has to make decisions, knowing that there are many people who do not agree with him; but with a sense of righteousness and justice he must make the adjustment. But he must do it. It is not a very pleasant position, I can assure you; but that has to be done.

I am sure that these men whom you have elected will stand together to have this quadrennium the most marked and outstanding of any of the quadrennia in our history. I shall pray to this end and stand by them in every way that is possible that the plans of this quadrennium shall be carried out to success. God bless them. I am sure you love them and will stand by them. The Church of the Nazarene is confronting some of the most important questions in our history. This is a time for the Church of the Nazarene to put on a strenuous program of holiness conventions throughout the entire connection. I believe you have chosen four men to lead you on to glorious success, and I rejoice in the fact that we are so beautifully united together. *I believe this General Assembly is one of the greatest that I have ever attended* (italics added).

Following the remarks of Dr. Goodwin, the entire assembly stood and sang "Blest Be the Tie That Binds." The third verse contained a message to the four leaders.

We share our mutual woes,
Our mutual burdens bear;
And often for each other flows
The sympathizing tear.
—JOHN FAWCETT

Never again should the church experience such a fracture in its Board of General Superintendents that could have its effect in the whole denomination. Little did the new general superintendent know of his role in seeing that this did not happen. The Board of General Superintendents would indeed have to become just that—a board—and Hardy C. Powers would play a major part in seeing this come about.

2

District
Superintendent

Dr. P. F. Bresee, who is generally considered the founder of the Church of the Nazarene, had at one time lived in the state of Iowa. There he had served as pastor in a number of Methodist churches. He left Iowa to move to California. It was a significant move in his life and equally significant for the church he helped to found. If he had not made the move, there might never have been a Church of the Nazarene; certainly he would not have had such a major part in it.

Now the man who had become number 12 in the line of succession that began with Bresee, made a move from California to Iowa. One wonders if he had not made that move whether he would ever have become a general superintendent in the Church of the Nazarene.

Hardy Powers left California to become pastor of the First Church of the Nazarene in Council Bluffs, Iowa. The district superintendent of the corn state, Rev. Jim Short, had been the prime mover in bringing this about. He had been to southern California as speaker for a meeting of preachers. He was especially attracted to two young pastors on the Southern California District and made up his mind he wanted both of them to serve as pastors on his district back in Iowa. One was Hardy Powers. The other was a close friend, Buford Seals. Seals was called to the First Church in Des Moines just six months prior to the call given Powers from Council Bluffs.

While pastoring in California, Hardy Powers had seriously considered pursuing further education. He was enjoying success in the pastorate but wanted to be as adequately equipped as possible. He couldn't decide what to do. In this period of indecision he sought counsel from a pastor who was somewhat older than he and consequently more experienced. The man he approached was Rev. D. I. Vanderpool of the Bresee Avenue Church of the Nazarene in Pasadena.

"Do you think I ought to go on to school and further the education I already have?" asked the young minister of Rev. Vanderpool.

There was a pause before an answer was given. The response was actually in the form of a question. "Do you want to be a general superintendent, or do you want to be a soul winner?"

The question startled him, but then he found his answer. "Of course, I want to be a soul winner."

"Then," replied Rev. Vanderpool, "further education is not what you need. Return to your church and win souls."

How D. I. Vanderpool explained this logic when later both served on the same Board of General Superintendents would be interesting to know. At any rate, the point was well taken. The last thing Hardy Powers was guilty of was a selfish ambition which could be out of the will of God. Of course, he wanted to be a soul winner. That was his one aim in life, and success at achieving this goal was his highest ambition. Accepting the Council Bluffs assignment was certainly within the framework of this purpose for life, and he rose to the task with a zeal and enthusiasm

20

which came to be identifiable traits in his personality and commitment.

Four and one-half years after Dr. Powers became a member of the Board of General Superintendents, D. I. Vanderpool became a member also. At the initiating meeting when Dr. Vanderpool was receiving his orientation, Dr. Powers, the chairman, rather dramatically announced that now he had concrete evidence that he had never aspired to the office he held. He was, of course, referring to the advice he had sought from Dr. Vanderpool years before.

The demands of his ministerial assignments never gave Hardy Powers an opportunity to pursue further studies. He became in a very real sense a self-made man through the self-imposed disciplines of much reading and study throughout life. In 1942 he was requested to go to Northwest Nazarene College in Nampa, Idaho, where he received an honorary doctor of divinity degree.

After some months in the Iowa pastorate a revival broke out in the church. It was a move of God's Spirit on the congregation which produced deep and lasting results. The growth which was evidenced during this period testifies to the intensity of the revival.

As to just how and when the revival started there are various explanations. Some of the congregation insisted it began in a prolonged prayer meeting which was conducted by the pastor himself. Rev. Powers was never really sure that the revival did begin just then. What was apparently a time of blessing in an extended prayer session for the people present was in reality a minor crisis for the young pastor.

The minister had requested his people to join him in the pews toward the front of the sanctuary. He himself came down from the pulpit and met with them there.

There were small racks attached to the backs of the pews, each rack designed to hold three Communion cups.

Rev. Powers called on his people to kneel and join him in prayer. He was standing between the first and second row of pews when he knelt to pray.

During the time of prayer the pastor laid his hand on one of the racks and thoughtlessly put one of his fingers through a hole made for holding a Communion cup. When he tried to pull his finger out it didn't budge. The hole was just small enough and his finger now swelled large enough that no amount of movement would release him. He struggled with it, but in vain.

Each time a prayer was concluded he called for another and still another. He needed time to extricate his finger. Finally with great effort and no little amount of pain he was able to free himself. The finger was tender and badly skinned.

He managed to keep his congregation from knowing of his plight in spite of a sore finger. The people, in turn, were refreshed and encouraged from the prolonged prayer session. But not the pastor. He didn't feel blessed at all.

Revival did break out, and the people pointed back to the very special prayer meeting led by their pastor who kept them on their knees in intercession as its beginning.

Positive things began to take place in Council Bluffs First Church. Membership increased from 168 to 260 during the years he served there. Sunday School had an average attendance of 164 his first year and 273 his last.

This happy, enthusiastic, and spiritually inclined young minister began to captivate the attention of Nazarenes over the Iowa District. The success at Council Bluffs obviously gave them reason to believe he was a coming leader in the church. Perhaps someday they might even have him as their district superintendent.

In 1936 Rev. and Mrs. Powers, along with their Council Bluffs delegation, attended the Iowa District Assembly. It was held in the town of Chariton. There they encountered a situation which later they would identify with striking similarities to that which existed at the General Assembly in 1944. The incumbent district superintendent found his position being threatened by a strong negative element which wanted his removal.

The vote was taken, and as predicted by many who were present, the district superintendent was not reelected. In fact, of the 172 people voting he received only 69 ballots in his favor, far short of the necessary two-thirds for reelection.

Nazarene church polity at that time did not provide for reelection with a yes or no expression on the ballot. Rather, the delegates were to simply write down the name of any elder they wanted for district superintendent. This made it somewhat easier for a district to effect a change when there was desire to do so.

Because of this write-in system, on the very first ballot, the one on which the district superintendent received only 69 votes, Hardy Powers learned that 57 people had written his name on their ballots. His election was almost inevitable, and by the third ballot Hardy C. Powers was elected district superintendent of the Iowa District of the Church of the Nazarene. He was just 36 years old.

The next eight years would be given to the shaping of the Nazarene work in Iowa in keeping with his style of leadership. They were good years, and the district responded well to the directives he gave. It was a period of significant growth. In 1936, when he was elected, the district reported 2,667 members. In 1944, when he left the district for the general superintendency, there were 3,786 members, a 40 percent gain.

It was a period in which the superintendent led the district in an aggressive church planting program. There was a net increase of 18 new churches during his tenure of service. He left the district with 69 church organizations.

Financially the growth was very pronounced. True, he became superintendent in the midst of the depression years and left when the economy was providing employment because of war demands. Nevertheless, the annual giving increase from $53,000 in 1936 to $211,000 in 1944 is noteworthy.

While Powers was shaping Nazarenes in Iowa, Iowa Nazarenes were also shaping him. This deserves explanation.

Iowa is in the very heart of the Midwest. There are many myths expressed concerning this section of the United States, particularly by those who live on either coast. It is true that traditional family and religious values run deep in this culture, traits that have lent themselves to a certain conservatism which finds its expression in many areas, including politics and religion. When you place an evangelical, theologically conservative church in the midst of this environment, certain conditions are apt specifically to identify such a church. This kind of conservatism is not to be confused with a restricted or limited outlook as far as mission or purpose is concerned. To the contrary, more likely than not it will be wrapped in an extremely aggressive and progressive program of outreach and expansion.

This is essentially what Hardy Powers found in the Midwest. What he saw he liked, and he identified with it. The value placed on this kind of conservatism would become one of his own trademarks throughout the rest of his ministry. Outward identification of this would be simplicity in taste and life-style accompanied with modesty in appearance, avoiding costly and gaudy extremes.

There were dangers in this, dangers which Rev. Powers avoided. Never did he or his family identify with legalistic trends which could easily emerge in such an atmosphere. Nor would the district at the time of his superintendency be known as anything other than a typical middle-of-the-road district of the Church of the Nazarene. It made reasonable sense to him for holiness to reflect conservative taste personally and corporately. He consistently employed this as a self-imposed rule throughout his ministry.

In applying this principle to his preachers, he would summarize his remarks by illustrating them with reference to a passenger train and its locomotive. His point was that the engine always went beyond the station so that the passengers would make it at least to the station. The locomotive is the minister and his wife. It is necessary, he felt, for pastors and spouses to be willing to go beyond what may be required of the laity so that the people who are following ministerial leadership will not lag too far behind.

For Powers, Sabbath observance was a case in point. One day of the week should be recognized as the Lord's day which would include no unnecessary purchases to be made on Sunday. The demands of travel, first as a district superintendent and even more so as a general superintendent where international time zones would be crossed and crisscrossed, sometimes made it difficult to respect one day of the week in such a traditional sense. But even here Dr. Powers was cautious, always going "beyond the station."

On one occasion he was with a ministerial colleague in a foreign airport. It was Sunday, but travel had in fact blurred away distinctives between days. The colleague stepped into one of the airport's duty-free shops and purchased a bargain wristwatch. Returning to Dr. Powers, he urged him to take advantage of the same opportunity. With an impish smile on the general's face (for never was he pharisaical and imposing about such matters) his reply was a gentle rebuke. "It is Sunday, you know."

The friend had forgotten, but Dr. Powers had not. Furthermore, it was important to him that he not forget.

He applied the "beyond the station" principle to the ministry. Particularly was this so in ordination services, in regard to the excessive use of jewelry by ministers and their wives, which he felt contradicted a conservative holiness life-style. Rather than preach about such matters, he simply felt the example of the ministry should suffice so that "passengers would make it to the station."

While there was a time in the Midwest when the above line of thinking carried this concept to an extreme, Powers never identified with those who did so. To the contrary, he even bucked these trends.

For example, the extremists wanted to impose a wedding ring ban not just on the ministerial couples but on Nazarene church members in general. Indeed, they succeeded at this in some areas. While some would have attributed such a position to Hardy Powers, one needs only to note that his widow still wears her wedding ring to this day to know that such an attitude was not a part of her husband's thinking.

As a member of the Board of General Superintendents during a time of great cultural change, Dr. Powers did find himself on the side of extremity, not so much because of a so-called jewelry matter but because of another principle which unfortunately found its expression in such a tenuous issue.

During the economic development period in the United States and other Western countries following

World War II, accompanying cultural changes began to emerge. There was a time when nearly all marriages included only a simple single ring ceremony at best. Two rings, one for the husband as well as one for the wife, were generally a financial strain for young couples, and double rings simply were not in vogue.

As strange as it may seem to some today, this became an issue of spiritual concern among many folks, particularly those in the holiness movement. Once the single and simple wedding ring matter was settled, now the question arose as to whether it included the husband's ring as well as the wife's.

This came to the attention of the Board of General Superintendents for direction, where a consensus was reached that no general superintendent would ordain a preacher who wore a wedding band. Dr. Powers had come onto the board at a time of tension and disunity amongst the general superintendents, and he felt such a crisis should never develop again. For the sake of maintaining an intact collegiality he would sustain the action of the board and implement the decision.

His friend G. B. Williamson was also now a member of the board, and a conflict developed between Williamson and Powers over this matter. Williamson obviously felt the position of the general superintendents was inconsistent, and he determined to bypass it. Regardless of how Powers may have felt about the specific issue itself, he considered himself bound to the consensus of the board.

Already Dr. Williamson had gone out on a limb, so to speak, and helped set the church's course on the ladies' wedding ring matter. At personal risk he had written a controversial editorial on the subject which had been printed in the *Herald of Holiness*. Eventually the wedding ring ceremony was even added to the wedding ritual in the church's *Manual*.

Now Williamson, in leading a crusade for consistency, determined to ignore the agreed upon ruling of the Board of General Superintendents. He would ordain ministers who wore wedding bands even if the others did not. Until the general superintendents as a board decided otherwise, Powers would not. This was only one of several such instances which developed during the time they served as general superintendents together.

Dr. Powers was sensitive about disagreements among the general superintendents being exposed to the entire church. Yet, if need demanded it, he was not timid in overruling a colleague if he felt it necessary. For example, Dr. Williamson had been in the country of Argentina where he conducted an ordination service for several national pastors who wore wedding rings. Later, when Dr. Powers was in Argentina he refused to ordain ministers unless they first removed their rings.

In Europe the sequence was reversed. First Powers had been there and then Williamson. The latter even commented while in Europe that because his colleague had overruled him in Argentina he could now do the same in Europe. The confused national Nazarenes found this difficult to understand. That Williamson eventually won this round there is no doubt. Whether the differences should have been imposed upon the people in such a manner there is some question. Dr. Powers always had concern that the church perceive the general superintendents as a board, able to resolve differences within the four walls of a conference room and then walk out a united body. Dr. Williamson's strategy was to find ways and means to garner support from the people when he felt strongly about a matter.

It must be repeatedly underscored, however, that in spite of what appeared to be conflicts between Powers and Williamson, the friendship between them survived.

They never lost respect for each other as leaders of their denomination. Perhaps this is wherein real unity lies.

In looking back, one has to conclude that the Midwest had a profound influence on the development of Hardy C. Powers as a church leader. His move from California to Iowa was a key factor in his life. Here he developed his philosophy of churchmanship, first as a pastor and then as a district superintendent. He was consistent in his "going beyond the station" philosophy all his life, never suggesting something for others he was not willing to do himself.

Going beyond the station meant just that: "beyond" but not "way beyond." Here he applied the brakes, and in doing so he managed to influence the Midwest as much as the Midwest influenced him.

One time, as the Iowa superintendent, he had been confronted by some on his district who were placing an undue and unscriptural emphasis on external matters. He began a practice at this time which he pursued throughout life of sharing major church concerns with his close friend and confidant, Buford Seals. The relationship between these two was unique, and those who knew both of them felt Dr. Powers always turned to Dr. Seals because of the latter's sense of humor. The friendship had its beginnings when both were young pastors in California. In the midst of this legalistic pressure Powers sought relief by talking the matter over with his friend Seals.

Dr. Seals made a suggestion. It was in jest, of course. He simply recommended that the two of them go out and form a new church, write their own rules, and then not let anyone ever change them by adding to or taking away. Dr. Powers responded immediately by saying if they did so it wouldn't be long until they would even be disagreeing with one another.

Perhaps that's the significant key to the success of Hardy Powers. He was a man of principle, yet possessed a charitable spirit toward others. His unique brand of leadership would be significant and needed during a crucial developmental period in the denomination he served. Eight years as a district superintendent proved to be preparation for the succeeding 24 years as a general superintendent.

3

Texas—California

When Hardy Powers was born in the state of Texas his father was working as a conductor on the Southern Pacific Railroad. The father had come to Texas from Tennessee when he was very young. His parents had died and left him an orphan. Friends who looked after him had brought him with them when they moved west in a covered wagon. As a young man he had married a Texas girl, and one child was born into the home. Shortly after giving birth to their only child the wife died, leaving her husband with a child to raise by himself. He married again and seven children were born to this union. Hardy was one of the seven. His parents were living in Walnut Springs, Tex. The date was June 7, 1900.

Hardy's railroad conductor father was religiously inclined and was active in the Methodist church. He was a loyal layman in his church, accepting the responsibilities of being Sunday School superintendent. He was also chairman of the church board.

The pastor was Rev. E. B. Hawk, a strong leader who exerted a positive spiritual influence on the entire family. Eventually Rev. Hawk was elected dean of the School of Theology at Southern Methodist University, where a library was named after him in his memory and honor.

Hardy's father expected his family to participate in the church's programs. Indeed, life for the family centered around their church. Its services were given priority in their lives.

Hardy grew up in east Texas. When a teenager he moved with his father and the rest of the family to the western part of the state. They settled in a town called Crawley. In the nearby town of Tahoka Hardy secured a job as teller in a bank.

Life in Tahoka became especially interesting to Hardy, for here he was attracted to a young lady named Ruby May King. Her father was the owner-operator of the local hotel which was located on a corner opposite the bank where Hardy was employed.

Miss King had a daily assignment given her by her father. She was to get the mail from the post office for the hotel. Now, the post office was located on a third corner in such a location that the young lady walked past the bank from the hotel to the post office and back again. Of course, there was the opposite corner from the bank which would have been just as close, but she chose to go by the bank each day instead.

Needless to say, the young bank teller looked forward to seeing the hotelier's daughter make those daily treks. He knew she had to be the girl for him.

During one of Hardy's noon hour breaks he was standing on the corner with two of his friends when Ruby walked by. As one might expect, she was the subject of conversation among the three young men.

"I'd sure not like to have to buy clothes for that girl," one of them said.

To which Hardy replied, "I wouldn't mind, for she's the girl I plan to marry someday." He could hardly believe himself what he had just said. Up until now he had barely ever even spoken to the girl. Apparently the hidden sentiments of his heart simply had to find expression. Not only was he surprised at himself, but his friends were equally shocked at his pronouncement.

In addition to seeing her on the corner on her daily walks, Hardy had been introduced to her in church. His sister, Lilly, had invited Ruby to join her in services at the Tahoka Methodist Church. Although a Baptist, Ruby had responded to Lilly's persistence and became a regular attender.

Lilly plotted how to bring her friend Ruby and her brother Hardy together. She told Ruby there was someone "special" she should meet, and an occasion presented itself when it was convenient to introduce them to each other. Ruby immediately recognized the someone "special" as the young teller in the bank who looked for her to pass by each day.

A friendship developed which intensified Hardy's feelings for the young lady. He became convinced he wanted her to be his wife. Although they had met, they were no more than acquaintances, and Hardy felt he was having considerable difficulty in capturing her attention in a way that might lead to a courtship. The occasional moments when they found themselves in situations that might lead to conversation, the starry-eyed suitor was so overcome with embarrassment he could think of nothing to say.

One such occasion occurred in the local drugstore where they happened to meet each other. Their eyes met, and they found themselves facing one another. Hardy desperately sought for words so that he might make conversation with the pretty young lady. The opportunity seemed ideal. As he groped for words his hands groped for something to steady him. Reaching out, he touched a gadget which was a type of slicer used to cut off the ends of cigars. These were standard equipment in drugstores in those days. The solidity of the slicer helped steady the stammering young man as he endeavored to make conversation with the girl.

The ice was broken. The conversation began to flow, and Hardy gained his poise. He continued to keep his hand on the cigar slicer while he talked, however. Now totally engrossed in conversation and likewise totally enraptured with the pretty young lady, he accidently stuck his finger in the hole where the cigars were placed to be sliced; and believe it or not, he pulled the lever, cutting off the end of his finger! It was a moment of panic and extreme embarrassment for him. If his purpose was to gain sympathy from Ruby, he certainly succeeded. One wonders when his finger got caught in a Communion cup rack later if he didn't have flashbacks to the drugstore in Tahoka, Tex., and the cigar slicer.

From then on it didn't take long for the acquaintances to develop a meaningful friendship which led to an active courtship on the part of Hardy. Frequently the two were seen together. Social life, of course, centered around the Methodist church, and both actively participated in all of the church's activities.

Not far from Tahoka, out in the country, was another little church. Young people in the Methodist church heard of a revival taking place in this rural church and decided to attend. They really knew very little about the church except that it was simply referred to as the Grasslands Church. They eventually learned it was affiliated with a very new and still very small denomination known as the Church of the Nazarene. Hardy and Ruby joined the young people for the night out at the Grasslands revival services.

Upon their arrival they found the church crowded to capacity. Some of the group would have to stay outside. Ruby and the girls volunteered to stay outside. They sat on car fenders straining themselves to see inside. The boys worked their way in and found places to sit in the church. The service was a lively one with lots of singing and testimonies. The visitors observed it all wide-eyed. Afterward on their way home, all agreed that "those Nazarenes sure did have a good time tonight."

It didn't take long for Hardy to propose to Ruby. She quickly accepted and they proceeded with plans to get married. Things had moved very rapidly. Actually, from the time he announced to his friends on the street corner that Ruby King was the girl he planned to marry until they made their vows to one another at the altar of the Methodist church, it was only six months. Even then Hardy showed traits of being a decision maker. He certainly demonstrated his ability to follow through once a decision was made.

A honeymoon trip took them to California. Once they arrived on the West Coast they fell in love with the area. They decided not even to return to Texas following the honeymoon but just to extend their stay in California indefinitely.

When they wrote back to family members of their intention, they sparked an interest in Hardy's father to consider moving west himself. He shared this possibility with his wife, who immediately agreed to the move. Soon all of them were settled near each other in the city of Alhambra in the southern part of the state.

Hardy and Ruby rented a house which happened to be only a block and a half from a Church of the Nazarene. On seeing the name of the church sign they remembered their visit to the Grasslands Church in Texas when they were just getting acquainted with one another. They recalled how "those Nazarenes sure did have a good time" that night. The memory was a pleasant one, and both Hardy and Ruby decided to visit this church in Alhambra.

Their first visit to the church was not a disappointment. These Nazarenes, too, certainly had a good time worshiping together. There was no question in their minds but that this would be their church home. The parents of Hardy likewise enjoyed the church and decided to make the switch from the Methodist church to the Church of the Nazarene. It turned out to be the beginning of a lifetime relationship for the Powers family which would continue into future generations.

Hardy's parents purchased a home close to where the young couple was renting. This meant they were all within walking distance of each other and of the church as well.

This full exposure to the growing young denomination called the Church of the Nazarene was a new but also full exposure to the Wesleyan doctrine of sanctification. Here they heard the teaching that this experience was to be received by faith instantaneously, but as a second work of grace, subsequent to conversion. The elder Powers was especially intrigued with this message. Whether it made much of an impact on the minds and hearts of Hardy and Ruby at that time it is difficult to say. Neither of them up until this point had experienced the forgiveness of sins as an initial work of grace, let alone giving attention to a second work of grace.

The father gave careful attention to sermons on the subject. His interest motivated him to seek out and read books on this theme. He was introduced to the books which were recognized as "holiness classics." One of them especially, *Perfect Love*, written by J. A. Wood, spoke to his heart. As he read further into the book he sensed his need for the deeper experience. He began to seek the "blessing." He longed for love to be made perfect in his heart and life. The thought of this was continually on his mind.

Interestingly enough, the elder Powers was not in a study or in the church when his faith reached out and claimed the experience for himself. He was walking down a sidewalk in Alhambra. The response to his faith was a sudden feeling of elation. He experienced joy and happiness which had to find expression. His family heard their father coming. Looking outside they saw him with one hand raised high, waving a handkerchief as he told them excitedly of what he had experienced. Hardy and Ruby were profoundly affected by this demonstration of faith.

The influences in the Methodist church in Tahoka, Tex., had been very spiritual ones. It is difficult to know why they had not as yet taken root in the heart of either Hardy or Ruby to prompt them to seek the Lord for themselves. Neither was really rebellious against religious teachings. They just simply seem not to have been awakened to the need for personal decisions in this direction. Now all of this began to change.

It was on a Sunday morning in the Alhambra church that Ruby made her move. She stepped out on her own and went to the altar of prayer. That morning she was beautifully and wonderfully saved as she received assurance of her own sins being forgiven. Hardy stayed back, resisting such a move. He would not be able to hold out for long, however.

Shortly after Ruby had experienced the grace of God in her own heart she encouraged Hardy to accompany her and a group of young people of the church to an open-air meeting which the church was conducting. It was to be held on one of the streets of Alhambra as a means of attracting passersby and preaching the gospel to them. But that day the message did more than go out to strangers who stopped and listened. It reached Ruby's young husband, Hardy. Then and there he responded to the invitation while his friends from the church gathered around and prayed fo. ' m. He repented, believed, and was saved. Often he would recall this occasion to mind as the crisis beginning of his spiritual journey.

This giant leap forward on the part of Hardy was very significant to Ruby especially. It meant that unitedly they could begin serving the Lord. And it meant a great deal to the Alhambra Church of the Nazarene as well. Now they had the participation of a splendid Christian couple as active laymen in the church. Once the start was made it was Ruby's intent that she and her husband would be all she understood they should be. This would include the practice of worshiping together at home as well as at church.

Ruby spoke to Hardy about a "family altar." The fact that she spoke to Hardy rather than him speaking to her was an embarrassment to him both as a husband and a young Christian. He recognized his wife was asserting leadership in spiritual matters, something he should be doing himself. This proved to be a very sensitive thing between them and could have led to a crisis in their marriage. He felt it was his role to assert leadership in the home and that he had failed in an important spiritual matter.

The crisis was met and the matter resolved. There would be a family altar and he would lead it. Later, in recalling this matter, Hardy's comment was that he felt "just so high" when he recognized his own failure at this point. There is more significance to this episode than meets the eye. It is inspiring to know that the practice established at that time was faithfully maintained throughout their marriage of 50 years. But more than that the shock effect of this incident brought about a radical shift by Hardy from being passive in his spiritual exercises to becoming a strong leader in such matters. The church which elected him to its highest office of spiritual leadership would have Ruby to thank for prompting him to develop his innate capacities for being a leader.

Indeed, Dr. Powers' own children have observed that it was their mother who saw the potential in their father for becoming the man he emerged to be. Outside of the Lord himself, Hardy's own family members became the strongest motivating factors in his life, especially his wife Ruby. It all began with the family altar episode.

Hardy and Ruby began to develop and grow in the things of the Lord. Praying together, worshiping together, and serving together, they experienced a close walk with God. Together they began to hear His voice speak to them of full-time Christian service. The sense of leading in this direction became especially strong during a series of revival services in the Alhambra church.

The evangelist for the services was Rev. Fred Suffield. Not only was Rev. Suffield an able preacher, he and his wife were well-known gospel songwriters. One of the songs his wife had written and which he sang in that revival meeting was "God Is Still on the Throne." The words seemed to speak directly to Hardy and Ruby.

> *God is still on the throne,*
> *and He will remember His own.*
> *Though trials may press us*
> *and burdens distress us,*
> *He never will leave us alone . . .*
> *His promise is true;*
> *He will not forget you.*
> *God is still on the throne.*

The words were meaningful and the revival in the church became a time of decision for the young couple. They had indeed heard the call of God. They were now confident of this. Furthermore, they were assured of God's providing care if they would embark on a venture of faith. The next step would require preparation if Hardy was to become a preacher. With the full support of his wife he enrolled in Pasadena College, a liberal arts institution of the Church of the Nazarene, and began to prepare for the ministry.

4

Husband—Pastor— Father

After deciding to live in California and not return to Texas, both Hardy and Ruby secured jobs with the Southern Bell Telephone Company in Alhambra. Hardy worked in an office while Ruby became a telephone operator.

When the parents of Hardy purchased a home, they invited their son and wife to move out of their rented house to a little one-room house with a kitchenette in it located on the back of the lot just behind their own home. This turned out to be a blessing financially when Hardy enrolled in college. There were, however, some risks with living so close to the parents.

The senior Powers did not see the potential drive in his son that Ruby saw in him. In fact, the father was never certain that Hardy would ever be much of a success in life. Ruby felt just the opposite and determined to shield her husband from the paternalistic protectionism of his father. But living in the little house helped ease the economic burden caused by Hardy's giving up his job in order to go to school. Ruby maintained her employment the entire time her husband was in college.

Hardy had attended a business college in Texas for a brief time which gave him the equivalent of one semester's work. He received credit for this at Pasadena College. It was a great day for Hardy and Ruby when the former bank teller from Tahoka, Tex., felt he was ready to embark on fulfilling his call.

He wanted to stay in the southern California area, so he approached the superintendent of that district to inquire of the possibility of getting a church to pastor. The response was disappointing. Superintendent J. T. Little replied that all of his pastorates were filled, and consequently no openings were available at the time. The news was disheartening to the young man.

Rev. Little, however, saw something in Hardy Powers that he liked. He sensed a determination to fulfill his call and use his acquired education some way or other. He told him of a church he was having to close for lack of interest and support. "If you want to see what you can do out there, you may do so," said the superintendent.

The response was immediate. "We'll take it," Hardy said. The excited and visionary couple moved to Cucamonga.

They found themselves in a small town, a small church, and a small parsonage with a woodshed attached to it. Frequently as general superintendent, Dr. Powers would make reference to his initial assignment, always calling it Cucamonga First Church. He then would let his hearers use their own imaginations to fill in the details as to what was implied by the reference.

People in the community were attracted to the young minister and his wife. They were an enthusiastic couple. They were also a happy couple when a son was born, Hardy, Jr. Attendance began to increase as the church showed signs of life again.

It was the pastor who was facing a spiritual crisis. He found his college classes and now his practical experience to be inadequate for his assignment. Furthermore, he began to discover spiritual deficiencies in his own life, and he didn't particularly like what he found.

He recalled his father's finding direction for himself in a time of crisis by reading from the holiness classics. He secured one of the volumes for himself. He read and studied it intently, determined he would make practical applications of its truths in his own life. The book he had was entitled *Holiness and Power*, by A. M. Hills.

Recognizing that his spiritual need was to be sanctified, he began to seek the experience. One Sunday morning when he went into his pulpit to preach he announced to his congregation that his subject that day was "Sanctification." He spoke of the deep conviction he had that he needed personally to be sanctified. He shared the hunger of his heart with his people. He then told them at the close of his message that he himself would be going to the altar to pray. He stated further he would be grateful if members of the congregation would join him to pray for him.

Upon completing his sermon he went to the altar. There he began to pray for his own spiritual need. After a few minutes he looked up to see who might have come to join him. There was only one, a man whom he described as "an old reprobate." The young pastor did not pray through to victory that day.

Determined to stay with it until he received the assurance of a heart made pure by the infilling of the Holy Spirit, he announced to his wife the next morning he was going into the woodshed to pray. Slipping out the back door of the parsonage and entering the door of the attached lean-to, there was a sense of resoluteness in his every move. With him on that day it would be "do or die." He made up his mind he would not leave until he knew beyond all doubt his prayers were answered.

He prayed all morning, over the noon hour, and on into the afternoon. At four o'clock he "struck spiritual fire." His consecration was complete and the sacrifice accepted. Faith overcame all doubts as he joyfully entered into the realm of the sanctified. What a great moment it was! What profound meaning it had for the future ministry of Hardy C. Powers! What significance that Monday afternoon had for the Church of the Nazarene! Throughout his lifetime he made frequent references to the woodshed as the place and that Monday afternoon as the time when he received the assurance of his heart made pure by the blessed baptism with the Holy Spirit.

Even today in retrospect one cannot help but wonder how many in the world would have been deprived of eternal spiritual benefits if it hadn't been for the determination of the young pastor of a little-known church in southern California to pay the price in prayer and consecration which would make him the pliable tool needed by God for the work intended for him. This was the basis for the motivation which eventually prompted him to lead the Church of the Nazarene in expansion all over the world. This experience helped secure him in his faith so that he could face many dilemmas, decisions, and crises as a church administrator, always finding a way to get through them. This new relationship with God even gave him strength to face the challenges of parenthood, especially when the demands of his calling forced him into long periods of separation from his family.

Having been sanctified wholly, Hardy Powers was known henceforth as a preacher of full salvation. He knew that what he had received was not just for a select few of those who might be chosen and called, or perhaps those who were designated by God to go into full-time Christian service, but that all who had experienced the saving grace of God could and should go on to the experience of holiness. Especially later as a denominational leader he called upon his ministerial colleagues not only to be assured themselves of a pure heart but to preach regularly and fervently on the subject, urging their congregations to claim the promises for themselves. He was convinced that the propagation of the holiness message as well as its preservation as a doctrine should be the primary aim and purpose of the Church of the Nazarene. Indeed, in his mind this was the only justifiable reason for the existence of the church. It was his firm conviction that if ever there was a letting down at this point, his church did not deserve to exist any longer.

When Dr. Stephen Nease was asked to serve as the first president of the new junior college to be established in the state of Ohio in the 1960s, Dr. Powers said to him, "Remember, whatever you do, make sure you establish a holiness college." This directive became priority with Dr. Nease not only in Ohio but also when serving as president of the denomination's school in Bethany, Okla., the seminary in Kansas City, and more recently at Eastern Nazarene College in New England. This response is indicative of how other church leaders accepted this same kind of direction from General Superintendent Powers.

In his preaching Hardy Powers clearly proclaimed that the experience of holiness should be evidenced by a heart made pure rather than the excesses of legalistic demands as outward evidence on the one hand, or charismatic glossolalia on the other. At this point he was firm that neither of these positions had biblical foundations. In his mind his denomination would continue to be a strong, dynamic movement as long as it emphasized the doctrine of holiness as basic, never allowing intrusions which might send the church careening in another direction. Because his leadership at this point was strong, he was able to help steer his denomination through some very difficult periods.

It should be noted that Cucamonga to this day has a strong congregation of Nazarenes. The demographics of the area changed greatly, with today's population being nearly 100 percent of Spanish descent. Today services in the Cucamonga Church of the Nazarene are conducted in Spanish, and the congregation is active and growing. Dr. Powers would be pleased with this development as it coincides beautifully with the philosophy of outreach he so openly avowed.

While serving in Cucamonga, Hardy Powers was ordained by General Superintendent J. W. Goodwin at the Southern California District Assembly in 1926.

Rev. and Mrs. Powers remained in this church for three years. They then accepted a call to the Compton church, also in southern California. Here they had another three years of significant ministry.

While in Compton Rev. Powers embarked on a helpful training adventure. He led the congregation there in a new church building program. All of this would prove to be valuable experience for him later as a church administrator.

During these pastorates two more children were born into the Powers family. First there was a boy named Dudley and then a daughter, Nona. These five (three children and the parents) would make the move together to Council Bluffs, Iowa, in 1930.

After the move to Iowa twin girls, Judy and Geneva, were born to Rev. and Mrs. Powers. Dr. Powers was already district superintendent when the twins were born. Needless to say, their arrival made them a very special subject of conversation on the entire Iowa District and even beyond.

Family came to be very important to Hardy and Ruby. The demands placed upon the father, first when serving as a district superintendent and then later as a general superintendent, became a great burden of concern to him. Prolonged absences left Dr. Powers with feelings of guilt. He felt he had let down one of his children, especially, in the fulfillment of his duties. Even as he lay dying he called for this one to come to his hospital room. He asked for forgiveness if he had in any way unintentionally neglected this one child. It was a poignant and touching moment, reflecting the great heart of a father who loved his family deeply.

During the difficult years of rearing their family Ruby stood loyally by her husband. They were both so committed to the will of God that in spite of problems which arose from time to time they kept each other's spirits buoyant and cheerful. Their love for each other intensified during these years. Ruby possessed strengths of her own which kept the family intact when her husband was absent. When the father arrived home, however, she always stepped aside, allowing him to assume his role as head of the house. Never were the children in doubt as to who was in charge when Dad was home. This system worked out well for the two of them all the while their children were growing up.

They faced a major family crisis during the years Dr. Powers was superintendent of the Iowa District. World War II had broken out, and their eldest son left home to serve in the armed forces. There was a prolonged period when the parents heard nothing from their boy, and loving parental instinct flashed warnings to them of possible danger. Then one morning they saw the headlines in their newspaper telling of a ship which had been hit and was sinking. Lives had been lost, and they were still in the process of looking for survivors. They knew their son was to have been on that ship. Now they understood their burden of concern.

Full of anxiety, the parents waited and prayed. Their concern went beyond the physical well-being desired for their son. This particular boy had been rebellious and had left home without leaving a personal testimony of being a Christian. He had deliberately rejected his parents' pleas for him to give his life to God, and he was determined to live as he desired. The forsaking of his parents' value system had led him into a life of sin. They agonized over the thought of his perishing in this tragedy at sea, knowing he was not ready to meet God.

The wait was long and their fears were not empty. Their son had been in great danger. In fact, he spent several hours in the water waiting to be rescued. It was a relieved and happy set of parents who eventually received word of their boy's safety.

Now they intensified their prayers for the boy. If God could save him physically, He could do the same for him spiritually. They held on in prayerful intercession for their son's salvation. What joy was theirs when he eventually was saved and answered his own call to preach. Hardy, Jr., supported by a wife who shares her husband's commitment to ministry as well as a family who are all active participants in the work of God, has enjoyed success as a pastor, having served some of the denomination's larger churches.

Spiritual concerns have always been primary with Hardy and Ruby Powers. This has been true whether dealing with the denomination they loved and served or in relationship to their children who have been dearer than life itself to these dedicated parents. In his quiet moments, often while alone in hotel or motel rooms, Dr. Powers expressed his thoughts on paper, frequently in the form of poetry. Consequently, he has left a legacy to his family worth more than a rich estate of stocks, bonds, and real estate. He has left his innermost thoughts and concerns. A burden he carried for the spiritual welfare of one of his children was strongly expressed in this piece he had written which was discovered among his papers after his passing.

I need You, Lord.
When heartache subsides from stabbing pain
   to dull, throbbing agony, beyond the reach of
      surgeon's knife or apothecary's balm,
When bright dreams, fair as newborn sunlight, fade into
   haunting nightmare, and hopes, long cherished, merge
      into the dank, dark "Slough of Never Return,"
When the heart, not the lips, says a final farewell
   to longings and prayers that for so long would not die,
When night no longer is approaching but has arrived
   and dropped its darkness over the soul,
When love's last faint call has been lost in the horrible,
   deceptive whisperings of sin as it smothers a soul,
When to move away from the place of tragedy
   brings no relief but rather intensifies the pain,
When because of long occupancy Gethsemane becomes
   my home, and in dim outline, a stone's throw away,
      men sleep, strangers to my burden,
Then I must place my hand in Thine, who has already
   sanctified that lonely spot before me, and pray,
"Lead me, lead me, lead me, Savior, lest I stray.
   And let not my heart forget all Thy benefits."

    After Dr. Powers was elected to the general superintendency the family continued their residence for two more years in Des Moines, where they had lived while he was superintendent of the Iowa District. Both Hardy, Jr., and daughter Nona had suffered from rheumatic fever as children, and now the same symptoms were appearing in one of the twins, Geneva. For that reason the family moved to Dallas, where they lived during the remaining 22 years of Dr. Powers' service as a general superintendent.

It should be pointed out that Dallas was selected for a residence over any other city in the South because of the friendship which had been cultivated between Hardy Powers and I. C. Mathis, who was then district superintendent of the Dallas District. This friendship had begun when I. C. Mathis had first visited the Powers home in Cucamonga, Calif. Hardy had climbed a tree to trim its branches but while there had experienced a big tear in his trousers. Just as he was preparing to come down to change, Rev. and Mrs. I. C. Mathis drove up to the parsonage. They had not met prior to this. They introduced themselves to each other, Mathis on the ground and Powers in the tree. Powers remained up in the tree, too embarrassed to tell his guest why he would not come down. The puzzled Mathis eventually left, thinking what a strange young man this Hardy Powers was.

It was the beginning of a lifelong friendship, one of several very special friendships which Dr. Powers cultivated and enjoyed. In fact, probably no person enjoyed his friends more than did Hardy Powers. Having someone in Texas he knew well who could look in on his family if needed while he was absent was a motivating factor in the move to Dallas.

Returning to Texas completed a cycle for Hardy and Ruby. Here they had been born. Here they had met and married. Life had taken them to California and then to Iowa. Returning to Texas would close the final arc of the circle. This was home.

5

Bridge Builder

Hardy Powers became the bridge that spanned two distinct leadership styles in the Church of the Nazarene. It might be suggested that he as much as anyone helped his church move, for lack of better terms, from an era of "natural" leadership to a more modern "professional" style of church administration. Because he himself possessed qualities of both styles, his brand of leadership was especially significant.

In 1983 the Nazarene denomination celebrated the 75th anniversary of its 1908 merger. As a part of the publishing house's participation in this event, M. A. "Bud" Lunn, the manager, commissioned a professor of Olivet Nazarene College to paint a mural in honor of the occasion. Mr. Harvey Collins, the artist, placed a portrait of Hardy Powers in a rather significant position in the mural, front and center of the colleagues whom he joined on the board in 1944. In a sense this mural says it all. Professor Collins, in his explanation concerning the mural, said simply, "General Superintendent Hardy Powers is the bridge to the next generation of leadership."

The mural, which has a prominent place for viewing at the denomination's international headquarters, will be a permanent reminder of this unique role Hardy Powers played in the history of his church. In short, he was the bridge between the Williams-Chapman era on the one hand and the Williamson-Young-Benner period on the other. Not to be overlooked are other leaders on either side of the bridge, but interaction with those named is especially significant, particularly in the developing "board concept."

When Dr. Powers was elected, R. T. Williams had served as a general superintendent from the time he was a young man. Not yet 33 years old when chosen, he had already served 28 years on the board. J. B. Chapman had been a member of the board since 1928. H. V. Miller had been on only since the preceding General Assembly, so he was still considered a relative newcomer. When one speaks of the era of "natural" leadership the more specific reference is to Williams and Chapman.

More often than not a great, successful business operation will trace its roots back to a founder who possessed qualities of natural leadership. The entrepreneur type who is strong and decisive is usually the kind to bring about success. Williams and Chapman would both fit this image. They were exactly what the church needed during its adolescent years of development. People everywhere leaned heavily on this kind of strong and dependable leadership. These men were deeply loved, but it could probably be added that by many they were lovingly feared. They shaped the church and gave it direction.

The parallel between the church and a developing business is seen when the business gets to such a size that no longer does the single entrepreneurial style of leadership carried on by the founder or his family fit. Growth requires the organization to move into a style of leadership where corporate decisions arrived at by consensus of a board are more desirable.

Historically it would appear that this is where Hardy Powers stepped into the pages of Nazarene history. Transitions would have to be made. Growth in the denomination would require development of managerial positions in the church to carry out directives to be given by a corporate board. The important thing would be for the board to find consensus and then act unitedly.

It needs to be pointed out, again following the business model, that the period of transition from "natural" to "professional" styles of leadership can often be very disruptive.

All four of the members of the newer team had qualities of both styles. In addition to Williamson, Young, Benner, and Powers there were others who contributed greatly in their own ways to help effect the transition. There was Dr. D. I. Vanderpool, whose tender spirit and loving manner helped ease the board through many disagreements. When Dr. Powers retired in 1968 he would leave, in addition to Samuel Young, his friends V. H. Lewis and George Coulter on the board. As newer members they would, as much as anyone, finalize the transition and bring about the kind of administration the church has today.

Drs. Williams and Chapman both passed away between the 1944 and 1948 General Assemblies. Drs. Miller and Nease passed away during the next quadrennial period. In a relatively short time Dr. Powers found himself to be the senior general superintendent. With the loss of so many in such a short time there was great concern over any future attrition on the board by death. When Dr. Powers would be introduced as "senior" general superintendent, he would always respond with a quip that he intended to remain senior for a long time. He did just that. For nearly 20 years he was the longest serving living member of the Board of General Superintendents.

Under the old regime, seniority had dictated the one to serve as the board's chairman. Dr. Williams had held this position for a long time. Now this responsibility fell on the shoulders of Hardy Powers. At the time he became chairman a certain amount of recognition went with the position. There came a time when the other board members felt this should not be the case. They viewed the chairmanship as a function to be shared and rotated rather than a position assigned by seniority. When the transition was made after Dr. Powers had been chairman for 10 years, it was not done without some misunderstanding and perhaps even hurt feelings.

He would not serve as chairman again until one year before his retirement. This request by his colleagues reflects the magnanimous collegiality which had emerged on the board. This meant that at the time of retirement, history records that Hardy C. Powers was the illustrious and esteemed chairman of the Board of General Superintendents.

Hardy Powers was so intent on the board's functioning corporately and unitedly that he apparently saw his leadership as chairman as essential to bringing this about. He felt keenly that in placing a harness on the team someone had to keep a tight rein on it. The other members didn't necessarily mind the harness as long as one was on him also.

Now, of course, it must be understood that just as it has been observed that major transitions from one era to another are not made without stress and some pain in the business world, it was equally true in the Church of the Nazarene. The four men—Powers, Williamson, Young, and Benner—would all have fit the previous period as well as the latter. Indeed, sometimes the harness on the team hung pretty loose. As far as Chairman Powers was concerned, double doors and soundproofing for the general superintendents' conference room were essential. He wanted differences to be resolved there, regardless of how heated the conversation might become, that they

54

might emerge a united body. It was during this time the power of veto was extended to each member of the board on certain decisions so that final conclusions would indeed reflect unanimous consensus.

One such occasion gives a case in point. Discussion was taking place regarding the restoration of credentials to a minister who had lost them on an immorality charge. The two-year waiting period had passed, and his case was up before the board for review. It turned out to be another time when Williamson and Powers found themselves on opposite sides of an issue. Williamson argued for restoration, Powers opposed it.

The decision would have to be unanimous, and Powers kept Williamson from achieving his desire. The debate between the two was rather heated and long. Late into the day Dr. Powers said to his colleague that when the sun came up the next day he would still be opposed to restoration in this case. The deadlock blocked the matter from further consideration.

Within six months word reached Dr. Williamson that the one in question had again left his wife for another. This, of course, left Dr. Powers' judgment in this particular matter undisputed. When they next met behind closed doors with the other general superintendents, Dr. Williamson characteristically said, "You were right, and I am entitled to a good swift kick."

Humor and a spirit of camaraderie overrode many differences and brought these strong individualistic personalities into an effective and efficient working unit. All of them deserve high marks for making this happen. Considering the kind of administrative genius possessed by each one, it must be concluded that in the final analysis they were great Christian gentlemen who acted on behalf of the church always rather than in the interest of self and personal concerns.

Probably the greatest test to this developing and now working relationship came about in 1964 at the Portland, Oreg., General Assembly, with the proposal of Dr. Williamson that a recommendation to establish two new junior colleges include a Bible college as well. Dr. Williamson felt keenly about the issue. Just as keenly did the other members of the board oppose the idea.

Not being able to secure the support of his colleagues, Dr. Williamson took the matter alone directly to the General Assembly. With a prepared speech in his pocket he walked down off the platform and proceeded to a microphone on the floor. It was a tense moment for the entire assembled body. It was also exciting. The debate that followed between Dr. Williamson on the floor and Dr. Benner, in particular, on the platform would be talked about for a long time to come. Another round would be chalked up to Williamson, for the Bible college was approved and is in full operation today.

This was not the last of the discussion, however, as far as the Board of General Superintendents was concerned. In their first full meeting following the General Assembly the soundproofed double doors would again be needed to contain what went on inside the conference room.

Dr. Powers asserted himself on the issue. It had been his great concern to maintain a strong, united image of the board to the church, and he felt Dr. Williamson had betrayed the other members of the board. The issue was not over the fact that they were divided with one for and the rest against as far as Powers was concerned. He even agreed that Williamson had the right to take his case directly to the General Assembly. What disturbed him was that this was done without the knowledge of the board. He felt damage to the board's effectiveness would take a long time to overcome. He further was concerned that those who enjoyed seeing this kind of fracture would relish it, and the repercussions could result in others following the Williamson model at other levels of leadership in the church. His words were hard and penetrated deep into the sensitive spirit of Dr. Williamson.

Not backing up on his conviction that a Bible college was right for the church but repentant over his seeming betrayal of his colleagues, Dr. Williamson offered his resignation. The general superintendents refused to accept his willingness to step aside and proceeded to put the crisis behind them. They accepted the directive of the General Assembly and began to set things in motion for the establishment of the Bible college. They also felt that since the idea was Dr. Williamson's he should help implement it.

Another sensitive matter was dealt with at that particular General Assembly which would affect three of the members of the board. A proposal was presented and accepted that no one could be elected or reelected to the general superintendency following his 68th birthday. This would bring about the retirement of Williamson and Benner at the following General Assembly as well as that of Powers. That it was difficult for Dr. Powers to understand and accept, it was no secret. He would turn 68 just one week prior to the next General Assembly.

In looking back, one is inclined to conclude that this major crisis relating to the Bible college, faced and resolved by the board, was the conclusion to the period of transition from "natural" leadership styles to the more enduring and now necessary professional corporate style which would mark the future for the church. There would be new problems once the transition was made. The individualism of the old style did result in a productive, growing church as the people rallied around and followed the leadership of strong personalities. The church would have to learn how to translate a new team concept into motivating the church for growth as successfully as had been experienced before. Size and growth demanded the change if for no other reason than to avoid cultish type loyalty to personalities rather than commitment to the main thrust of the church.

The Church of the Nazarene had now grown up and become a recognized denomination in the world. The challenge of the future would lie in the success of a strong Board of General Superintendents acting corporately and decisively in planning for the future. In 1968, having just turned 68, Hardy Powers, along with two of his colleagues, G. B. Williamson and Hugh Benner, passed their gavels along to a newer and younger team of general superintendents. The bridge had been built, and the church faced the future assured that God, who had led so successfully since that fateful 1944 General Assembly in Minneapolis, would lead on into the future as well.

6

A World Vision

As strongly as Hardy Powers promoted unity on the Board of General Superintendents, he was not without fault in expressing his traits of individualism in making some unilateral decisions. This was particularly true in the mission enterprises he promoted outside the United States. That he was a leader for a world church there can be no doubt. During the time he served as general superintendent he was directly responsible for much of the aggressive expansion of the church's mission ministry.

In 1948 Dr. Powers delivered the Sunday afternoon missionary address at the General Assembly. He believed in a literal fulfillment of the Great Commission. "Since we are highly privileged," he said, "we have some obligations. We are obligated to the lost of the earth. . . . I believe that it is gloriously possible, if we utilize everything that we have at our command today, to evangelize our generation and to preach the gospel to the far corners of the earth."

He then proceeded to use his administrative skill and ecclesiastical authority to move the church out into the far corners. It must be remembered that he embarked on this aggressive program of mission expansion when the denomination was barely 40 years old. This makes the results all the more significant.

In its summary of his life's achievements at the time of his passing, the *Herald of Holiness* listed the countries where the Church of the Nazarene was directly ministering as a result of his leadership in opening these fields. They are Alaska, Bermuda, Bolivia, Chile, Cuba, Denmark, European South Africa, Haiti, Hawaii, Papua New Guinea, New Zealand, Okinawa, the Philippines, Sweden, and West Germany.

Of these fields it should be noted that the work did not take root in Sweden as Dr. Powers had envisioned it might. Endeavors are being made once again, and it is believed that seed sown will eventually spring forth into a viable church plant. At the time initial plans were made, Dr. Powers proposed the church send his son-in-law and daughter to pioneer the work in Sweden. But the plan was vetoed by his brethren on the Board of General Superintendents. The concern was expressed that such a move might reflect a conflict of interest which would be unacceptable to the church generally. The qualifications of the son-in-law would not be questioned, as demonstrated in his present success as a district superintendent in the church.

Added to the list should perhaps be the Netherlands, as the beginnings of the church there would be a direct offshoot of the opening in West Germany. For that matter, when the church was planted in Germany the denomination was present in only one other country on the European continent, Italy. The fact that in addition to Italy, Germany, Denmark, and the Netherlands, the church is today in Switzerland, France, Spain, and Portugal as well would undoubtedly be traced back to the initial vision Dr. Powers had for the continent of Europe.

To be faithful to this story as well as to all members of the Board of General Superintendents at the time and as his biographer, it must be pointed out that a significant move in this writer's life was a result of what was apparently a unilateral decision on the part of Dr. Powers. In the fall of 1957 he approached my wife and me, asking if we would consider an overseas assignment. In December of the same year he specified Germany as the place he had in mind. Upon acceptance of the directive I was in Kansas City when the Conference on Evangelism was being held in January, 1958. Dr. Powers requested our decision be kept quiet until he could formally announce it at the conference.

He did it typically Powers style. It was dramatically presented, and the moment was emotionally charged. Not only would I not forget it, but to this day I am frequently approached by those who say they were present on that memorable occasion—and that is now over a quarter of a century ago.

Word was later leaked to me that the next meeting of the Board of General Superintendents was an occasion when, this time, Dr. Powers was reprimanded. Apparently he had not clued in his colleagues on his plan, and they were as surprised as was the rest of the church. The decision having been announced, the board really had no alternative but to go along with it. This writer has often wondered what course life would have taken for him if Dr. Powers had informed the board of his plans. Would they have vetoed them or approved them? It is all history today, and it seems a similar question might be asked—if G. B. Williamson had endeavored to clear his Bible college speech beforehand with the board, what might have happened?

Much of what Dr. Powers did in leading the church in an aggressive program of expansion was given detailed administrative assistance by what was then known as the Department of Home Missions. At the same time the church had a Department of, first, Foreign Missions, and later, World Missions, which was in the minds of most the logical administrative department for all mission activity.

Of course, a certain amount of expansion led by Dr. Powers was assigned to the traditional missions department, but a great deal of it was placed under the Department of Home Missions. Projects started in places like Alaska, Australia, New Zealand, European South Africa, and northern Europe were assigned to Home Missions. They came to be known as overseas home mission fields.

No one really seemed to challenge this administrative channel, although occasionally questions were raised to try to improve the understanding of it. At first it was noted these were primarily English-speaking countries. It was then assumed that this was the rationale for overseas home mission works. But when West Germany was placed under the Department of Home Missions this explanation was no longer valid, since the language in Germany is German, not English.

It was then thought that perhaps this administrative course had racial overtones to it. This had to be rejected because the Black work in the United States was also under the Home Mission umbrella.

In a rare moment of candor Dr. Powers confessed to this writer the real reason why he had chosen this route in fields where he was personally involved in establishing the church. The secretary of Foreign (World) Missions was his personal friend. The friendship, however, did not include unity between them on mission philosophy. Dr. Powers felt his friend was too conservative, and this conflicted with his own aggressive, risk-taking, adventuresome approach to missions. The bottom-line interpretation of all of this was that Dr. Powers felt he could free up more funds for his mission entrepreneurial projects in this manner than following the usual channels.

The fact that Home Missions did not have a highly structured policy for its overseas work was also highly palatable to Dr. Powers. This way he would not be hindered in his own sometimes unconventional, even unorthodox modus operandi. He interpreted this to mean he didn't really have to go through anyone to do what he felt needed to be done.

It is doubtful that Dr. Powers used the term *internationalization* as it is being frequently employed by Nazarenes today. However, he would have to accept major responsibility for leading the church philosophically in this direction. At the time of his retirement he was interviewed by a newspaper reporter. He clearly pointed out that in his appraisal of the church he saw it accepting a world assignment which is all-embracing. "It crosses the color line," he said. "More people are dark-skinned than light-skinned, and if we are going to have a world operation, we are just going to have to remember that it includes all people."

His own lifetime of travels would eventually take him to all seven continents, every state in the U.S.A., and many islands of the seas. He was one of the first to take advantage of air travel extensively as a time saver. He had the privilege of being a passenger on the first jet plane that flew from Johannesburg to Rome. His travels opened doors for many exciting adventures.

One of the countries in which he was instrumental in opening mission work for the Church of the Nazarene was Papua New Guinea. After making an initial exploratory trip to that country, he captured the imagination of Nazarenes everywhere in relating details of his adventures there. It was at a time when this little nation was just opening to the outside world. It was exciting news as word began to filter out, of tribes being discovered which no one even knew had existed. There were, of course, people there who had not seen Westerners before, and consequently unaccompanied trips into the interior were at great risk. Australia had been given the task of administrating this country following World War II. Under their sponsorship the country was being opened for Christian missions. Dr. Powers wanted his church to respond to this unique opportunity; thus the exploratory trip.

He flew on commercial aircraft first to Port Moresby. From there he shared the cost of a chartered, small, single-engine airplane with a Catholic priest. Their destination was the rugged highlands of the interior.

Taking off from Port Moresby, they soon found themselves facing what the pilot called a "stuffed cloud." These were mountain peaks, he said, surrounded by white, fluffy clouds which obscured the tops of the mountains. The pilot could take no chances flying through a cloud, lest he find a mountain peak inside. All of this meant there would be sharp banking of the little airplane in order to avoid trouble.

The experience was frightening to say the least. This was true for both Dr. Powers and the Catholic priest. Each time the plane banked sharply to avoid another "stuffed cloud," the priest would cry out, "Holy cow." Dr. Powers didn't know whether to be afraid or to laugh. Another sharp turn and there was another "Holy cow." Now the general superintendent did seek an appropriate response. All he could think of was "Amen." The entire trip became punctuated with first "Holy cow," always followed by a fervent "Amen."

As a result of this exploration the church responded to his recommendations to open work in the New Guinea highlands. What was then the Department of Foreign Missions nominated Sidney and Wanda Knox to this pioneer assignment, and they were appointed by the General Board. The beginnings were impressive. In the very heart of that country a mission station which would have a far-reaching influence was established. Shortly after this was started tragic word was received of Sidney Knox's illness which led to his untimely death. But other missionaries were there by then, and the church was firmly planted and began to take root. The government not only requested but required the Church of the Nazarene to open both medical and educational work along with the evangelistic thrust of the mission in the country.

The medical work included a 100-bed hospital to meet the needs of the Kudjip Valley. The Nazarene Women's Missionary Society (later known as the Nazarene World Mission Society) made the raising of funds for the project their special assignment. Enthusiasm ran high as the entire denomination rallied behind the goal which was initially established at $400,000.

An important ingredient to the dynamics of this project was the exciting announcement that Dr. Powers' own son Dudley and his wife had accepted the assignment of spearheading the medical facility. Dudley was completing his medical training which had included not only an M.D. degree but a degree in dentistry as well. The qualifications were superb for the assignment. It was a happy day for the general superintendent when he and Mrs. Powers saw their son and his family leave for Papua New Guinea.

Hardy Powers had the unique capacity of sharing his experiences in dramatic sermons he prepared and delivered upon returning home from an overseas assignment. The "holy cow" story is a case in point, a story that was shared coast to coast and is remembered by many to this day. His presentations were more than just the relating of incidents. It has often been observed that Dr. Powers, in using his missionary experiences as illustrative material, was a master at telling these stories. The effectiveness of his presentations was enhanced by his sense of timing as an orator. He could hold an audience spellbound for long periods of time. Not unaware of this talent, he used it frequently to share his own vision for the church reaching the "far corners" and thus gained support for missions from the broader Nazarene constituency.

Wherever he went, to district assemblies, preachers' meetings, or local churches, Nazarenes eagerly awaited an exciting word on the work of the church in some country their general superintendent had recently visited. No missionary could recount with greater enthusiasm details relating to the missionary enterprise of the church.

When under his leadership the church was planted in West Germany, Dr. Powers developed a sermon titled "The Master Weaver." He used incidents relating to the church in postwar Germany which reflected God having been at work in many lives in many places which all fit into a pattern that emerged as the church was finally established in this European country. Throughout his delivery his audience would find themselves moving in and out with the Weaver's deft hands until the final pattern came into focus. To preachers especially his sermons became models of how real-life situations can be applied to stir and motivate audiences.

Philosophically he believed the ultimate key to a successful missionary venture was found in the initial personnel selected for a given project. He gave as much time and thought to this selection as to any other detail. In addition, he became personally acquainted with a new field by a personal visitation of it before any missionaries were sent out. In the process of a lifetime he became something of an expert in world affairs. Always he found adventure in his travels, and always he found occasion to share the excitement of his experiences with others.

Preaching in foreign countries through an interpreter was never a difficult thing for Dr. Powers. Sometimes it was challenging, but never a problem to him. Those who intepreted for him remember his staccato delivery in the use of short sentences. He seemed to be able to develop a rhythmic interplay between himself and an interpreter so that listening to him became an enjoyable experience wherever he went. This talent made him a welcome pulpit guest all over the world.

On one occasion he was preaching in a foreign country on the subject of tithing. In prior conversation he had encouraged the missionary to urge the people to tithe. He firmly believed that a principle valid for people in one country was just as valid elsewhere. Furthermore, he felt the ultimate aim for the church everywhere was eventually to be totally self-supporting. He saw tithing as a necessary practice in order to reach this goal.

In this particular country the concept of tithing was resisted. It was much more comfortable to receive subsidy indefinitely from the general church and thus not place undue requirements on the national church. The missionary had shared this problem with his general superintendent, so now Dr. Powers had felt his response should be in the form of a sermon on tithing.

The service was lively with frequently heard "Amens" and "Praise the Lords" punctuating the preacher's remarks. A satisfied and much pleased general superintendent spoke of the positive response of the people and used this to admonish the missionary. "See," he said, "preach on tithing and the people here, too, will respond. Simply give them Bible truths on the matter.

The missionary himself had not interpreted the sermon but had requested one of his capable bilingual pastors to do so. The missionary had simply listened. But, of course, he understood both languages. He could hardly contain himself from laughing out loud during the message, and now he was really enjoying what his general superintendent was saying to him. They knew each other well, and the missionary was enjoying the fact he would be one up on Dr. Powers.

"You know what you preached on today, don't you, Dr. Powers?" asked the missionary.

"Of course," he replied. "I preached on tithing."

"No," continued the missionary. "Today you didn't preach on tithing. Today, your subject was 'God is love.' "

What had taken place was this: When the speaker began to speak on the delicate subject of tithing and the interpreter realized the direction the sermon would be going, he changed the theme from tithing to one of his own liking. He then proceeded to interpret Dr. Powers' remarks into a sermon of his own on the subject "God is love." This explained the enthusiastic response from the audience. Dr. Powers took great delight in telling this story on himself and did so many times.

At another time when he was visiting Africa, Dr. Powers expressed to the missionaries a secret wish of his. He wanted the experience of living, sleeping, and eating like one of the typical Africans. The request was considered and details worked out so that his wish might be fulfilled. He was to move into the kraal and remain there overnight. All went well, and the next day to round out the experience it was arranged for him to attend a typical feast of the area.

At the celebration he observed a big pot over a fire and was informed that stew was cooking in the pot for the feast. Dr. Powers inquired of the missionary if it would be all right for him to eat the stew. He was assured it would be fine.

Dr. Powers stood around with the others waiting to be served. He was near the cooking pot and leaned over to peer inside. There he saw an African wildebeest being cooked, head and all. To him it seemed as though the eyes of the wildebeest were staring right at him, pleading for rescue. It was more than he could take. He simply couldn't bring himself to eat any of the stew. His comment was that the wildebeest had the most discouraged look he had ever seen.

His world missionary interests opened doors for many opportunities for Dr. Powers to meet people of renown. Shortly after World War II he made an official visit to Japan. He asked General Church Treasurer John Stockton to accompany him. While in that country Dr. Howard Hamlin, then a medical surgeon serving in the U.S. Army occupational forces, was their host.

Gen. Douglas MacArthur was the commander of the army of occupation in Japan and was recognized as a leading world figure because of this role. He had made his now famous appeal for Christian missionaries to that country to play a significant part in the rebuilding of the nation. Dr. Hamlin was able to arrange for a private interview to take place between the general and Dr. Powers. It was scheduled to last no longer than 20 minutes. Much to the amazement of the waiting Hamlin and Stockton, the entire interview lasted two hours.

The need for missionaries in Japan was discussed. But it went beyond that. The two men found several common interests and concerns about which they could converse with meaning, and a bond of understanding between them emerged in that brief time. Dr. Powers often observed that he felt Gen. Douglas MacArthur was the strongest human personality he had ever met.

Another world figure with whom he had an interesting and meaningful encounter was King Hussein of

Jordan. The king was very young at the time. But when the appointment was made he and this senior church leader enjoyed instant rapport. They became so engrossed in conversation that the king had to be reminded of a significant meeting he was expected to attend with a rather large group of desert chieftains. To Dr. Powers he said, "Come along and be my guest." Together they rode to the large palatial hall where Dr. Powers was honored to sit on the dais next to the king for two hours or more. "It was the most remarkable meeting I ever attended," commented Dr. Powers.

This capability of communicating with national and international leaders led Dr. Powers to enjoy a special relationship with King Sobhuza II of Swaziland. This monarch had been educated at Oxford University in England. Officially he ruled his country from a fine office complex in his nation's capital. Privately he observed traditional customs, living with his many wives in the royal kraal complex.

The friendship between the two men was sealed when shortly after the war the general superintendent was beginning what turned out to be a 12-year jurisdictional assignment in Africa. Upon visiting the country of Swaziland he learned that World War II shortages even affected a royal household. For King Sobhuza this meant his Buick automobile lacked some necessary parts and, consequently, was not running.

Back in the United States Dr. Powers contacted his friend Bud Lunn, then an executive with General Motors in Detroit, who in turn secured the necessary spare parts. Soon they were on their way, and a grateful king never forgot. Each time he was there Dr. Powers had easy access to His Majesty's presence. This resulted in much more than a mere acquaintance with one another.

This author will never forget one of Dr. Powers' visits to Germany while I was serving the church there. One of our original German pastors who did not remain long with us insisted on Dr. Powers visiting his city and his church. He wanted to impress the general superintendent and went to great lengths to do so. Obviously his congregation of seven members would hardly make an adequate impression, so he decided to use some political connections he had to set up an appointment between his church leader and the mayor of the city. Admittedly, the title "Oberburgemeister" carries some significance in Germany over and against just "Burgemeister." The city was made up of approximately 400,000 people, and we were to visit the "Oberburgemeister." Even this young missionary was a little excited over the prospect, but obviously the general superintendent was not.

Dr. Powers had just enjoyed his unusual visit with King Hussein of Jordan. "What's an Oberburgemeister?" he asked. I tried to explain that this was the equivalent to a British lord mayor. Still he was unimpressed. But he did go through with the interview. Rather to the surprise of both of us a whole battery of reporters was also there. What kind of word about this distinguished visitor our host pastor had shared with both the mayor and the press corps we were never sure. Whatever it was, it worked. Flashbulbs popped, questions were asked, a gift from the mayor was given, and all seemed to go well. Again Dr. Powers proved he was equal to the occasion.

However, some probing questions were asked about our church in that particular city, including how large our congregation was. The next day as we were leaving by train, I purchased a newspaper to see what got into print about our visit at city hall. There it was on page 3 under the headline "Church Prince Visits His Seven Local Members." I had great fun referring to my guest as His Highness, the church prince, for the rest of his visit.

No record was kept of the miles Dr. Powers traveled while general superintendent. One can only conclude there were many. He moved in and out of countries the world over like some move in and out of counties in America. He made many friends for his Lord and his church. His vision was great, and he was able to get many to share the vision with him. The result is a church today that reaches into more than 75 areas of the world.

7

Truth and Principle

Dr. Powers made his decisions in life guided by certain principles. It is difficult to spell out these axiomatic rules of his, for there is no record of his ever writing them out for himself. Yet those who worked close to him soon became aware that he worked within such a framework. In looking back and reviewing actions he took as well as conversations various persons had with him, some conclusions may be made which would aptly describe not just how Dr. Powers approached administrative situations but why he decided as he did in these matters.

Loyalty to Christ was obviously foremost with him. This was followed close behind with loyalty to his church. When a nephew of his, a young minister with great promise and one who probably was most similar to his Uncle Hardy in mannerisms and preaching style, decided to leave the Church of the Nazarene to assume leadership in a newly formed religious group, Dr. Powers took great exception to the action. The nephew pointed out what he felt to be nonspiritual trends in the church as justification for what he was doing. The response of Dr. Powers was a sharp rebuke. He felt the attitude of his nephew was far less exemplary of the holiness position than the so-called nonspiritual trends for which he had concern.

Indeed, attitude was of great concern to Dr. Powers. He never wanted to do anything but reflect a holy attitude himself, knowing that such was important to maintaining integrity in his own Christian character. This basic concern gave the outward impression sometimes of a laissez-faire approach to some administrative problems. But in reality this concern for attitude was more than likely the basis for it. He simply felt that impulsive over-reaction might stir responses which could hinder ultimate solutions to problems.

Whenever approached by someone in the church about a matter, he would give plenty of time for it to be talked out, not by him but by the one who approached him. Many can remember his listening ear and the conclusive remark, "Now, what was your problem again?" It was obvious strategy. He knew that the time allowed in all probability would make it possible for the one with the problem to find his or her own solution simply in the process of talking things over.

This same principle applied to letter writing. How many frustrations were vented against Dr. Powers because answers to postal inquiries were often late in coming. This was not careless administration as many surmised. Here again it was strategy. He often said that half the problems expressed in letters will have found their own solutions before an answer could ever be formulated.

He had a great capacity of being able to draw on a story from his memory to fit a particular situation. He used stories and anecdotes to ease tensions. He was also a master of the use of quips. These one-liners more likely than not were also an expression of his philosophy. When a young district superintendent sought advice on dealing with a minister who was creating difficulty on his district, Dr. Powers' reply was for the superintendent to remember the scripture "And it came to pass." True enough. In due time this that had come did indeed pass. The pastor moved on.

There were some situations which he felt would become more complex than ever if too much time was spent in unnecessary idle conversation about them. Much to the distress of his colleagues on the Board of General Superintendents, especially when he was serving as chairman, he would come into the meeting at the last minute, thus avoiding unnecessary preliminary conversations.

Usually his routine for attending these meetings included an overnight trip from Dallas to Kansas City by train. He would then request his friend Bud Lunn of the publishing house to join him for breakfast. Time was then spent with Mr. Lunn right up until the hour for the board meeting to begin. In the meantime the routine also included frantic phone calls from Dr. Benner, then secretary of the board, who would be contacting the publishing house to see if anyone knew anything about their chairman. This timing of arrival at the last minute was characteristic of Powers. Needless to say, it was a characteristic that wasn't always appreciated by his colleagues. Probably they would not agree with his reasoning for being late.

Many will recall that timing was a trademark of Dr. Powers as far as public services were concerned. Those who remember him can see him even yet coming onto the platform late, usually during a song service after the meeting had commenced. Whether this was strategy or adhering to a personal principle it is difficult to know. It will be recalled that the movement onto the platform, the handshakes, and the greetings did indeed serve as a type of preliminary introduction of the guest speaker.

On one occasion Dr. Powers was to participate in a ribbon-cutting ceremony for entering a new church building to be followed by a service of dedication. The crowd had gathered before the ribbon. The people wanted to go on into the church and get their seats and really didn't quite understand the delay in cutting the ribbon. There was some shoving and jostling about. The pastor, likewise, was in a near state of panic, for the general superintendent was nowhere to be found. At three o'clock promptly (the time scheduled for the service to begin) Dr. Powers arrived, cut the ribbon, and walked on into the church as planned. The pastor expressed amazement at the seeming poise and unconcern over a last-minute arrival on the part of his special guest.

One district superintendent recalls vividly this unflappable nature as to exact timing when driving Dr. Powers to an airport to take a plane. It was not a large airport. They parked the car and waited there for the plane. While engrossed in conversation they watched one aircraft come in and leave. They then went to the counter for Dr. Powers to check in. The agent said, "Why, sir, that was your plane that just left." This was no problem to Dr. Powers. If he missed one, there would always be another.

This writer and Dr. Powers were on an airplane together flying from Germany to Copenhagen, Denmark. Because of fog in Copenhagen we were unable to land. On the intercom the pilot announced we were flying on to Stockholm, Sweden. Dr. Powers was delighted. I was anxious, for I knew a congregation had gathered in a little church in Denmark waiting for us to come for a service. The general superintendent's pleasure in going to a city and country he had never visited before could not be contained. "We'll hire a car and a driver," he said, "and explore Stockholm for a possible new opening for the church." These were indeed the circumstances that eventually led to sending a couple into Stockholm to try to establish a congregation there.

It was this ability to accept altering circumstances as possible providential leadings which made it possible for him as a world traveler to face minor crises so calmly. A call from him in Spain telling of a flight schedule change which would bring him from Madrid straight to Frankfurt, Germany, meant this information would have to be relayed to the missionary in Italy who was waiting for him there. "It may be better this way," he said, "—if the missionary comes to me rather than my going to him."

The trip to Sweden left the two of us in a strange place unexpectedly over the American Thanksgiving holiday. We were stranded in Stockholm due to bad weather and were assigned by the airline to a small hotel about 15 miles out of the city due to overcrowded conditions in Stockholm itself. We decided to treat ourselves at least to a good Thanksgiving dinner. We would have it, at his request, sent to his room where we would eat.

During this period Dr. Powers was on a toasted cheese sandwich diet. Probably it had nothing to do with his health. He merely liked toasted cheese sandwiches and felt safe in eating them, particularly in foreign situations. For example, in their high-level conference in Frankfurt the missionary from Italy and Dr. Powers had feasted on toasted cheese sandwiches while they talked things over. Later in our home in Germany he had requested my wife to fix a toasted cheese sandwich for him rather than to prepare any other kind of meal.

Now it was Thanksgiving Day in Sweden and we were confined to a small, out-of-the-way hotel. I was determined we would not have toasted cheese sandwiches, even though turkey was probably out of the question. He agreed to let me order. The problem was that the menu was written only in Swedish, and we could find no one in the hotel who could speak either English or German (my second language).

I studied the menu, carefully pointing out to the waiter what I thought to be two orders of steaks. When our dinner arrived we each had a small piece of fish on our plates, and that was all. To me our Thanksgiving was a disaster, but not to Dr. Powers. He saw it as just another adventure, perhaps a story to relate someday. And perhaps there would even be a sign of providence in it.

Come to think of it, he probably was wiser than I knew. Now I am the one who can relate the event and laugh about it. Furthermore, it was a lesson to be learned on how he looked upon the unexpected and unanticipated events of life. "And it came to pass." The crisis came, but it also passed and is now behind us. Actually, it is a good way to face life.

The Stockholm stopover caused a delay in Dr. Powers' return to the United States. He was due in Chicago for the dedication of a new building which had been erected by the First Church of the Nazarene there. The superintendent of the Chicago Central District and the pastor of the church were counting on his presence for this service. The unexpected extra travel had made it impossible for the general superintendent to keep his clothes pressed, and he felt he could not dedicate that church in the clothes he had with him unless they were pressed. He prepared a telegram to the effect that he could not dedicate the church in Chicago, explaining the reason why. This was sent to the district superintendent. The result was that the superintendent met Dr. Powers at the airport with late Saturday afternoon after-hour arrangements made for the guest speaker to have his suit pressed. An unruffled general superintendent met the appointment and dedicated the church. But he did have a pressed suit. Surely a subtle strategy achieved for him his desired aim.

It must not be thought that Hardy Powers was careless or derelict in performing his duties. He simply felt that little was to be gained if one responded to pressure in all he did. Not long before he died he made the observation that it doesn't take very long to live a life. Life should then be deliberate, well paced, and enjoyed. It should also represent the best of which one is capable by the grace of God. His prayer for his children was:

> O Lord, help the children to be right
>   rather than rich,
> And help them to be good rather than great.

For himself as well as his family he prayed:

> O Lord, help us so to live
>   that it is easy for good men to be good,
>   and it is hard for bad men to be bad.

He often stated that it is one thing to have a philosophy of life, but it is quite another thing to put that philosophy to a test. For example, he felt that pure hearts made it possible for people to disagree agreeably. He had many opportunities to put this conviction to a test.

One day he was in conversation when concern for the youth of the church was brought up. He quickly responded by saying he was not afraid for the future as far as the present generation of young people was concerned. Conversation was centering around some signs of rebellion to be observed in many young people. This was in the early part of the so-called turbulent 60s. Dr. Powers then went on to say that these young people were not rejecting Christ, but many of them were rejecting "churchianity." He used this point to distinguish between Christianity and what he called "churchianity," the latter reflecting an institutional loyalty rather than affections being centered on the person of Christ.

Dr. Powers developed an interesting philosophy about leadership. He observed that leaders emerge in any group of people. "There are even leaders among leaders," he was heard to say. One assumes he was speaking of the Board of General Superintendents.

His life was enriched because of his friends. In fact, he enjoyed several close friendships. He was known to call B. V. Seals frequently by long distance, often having lengthy conversations with him. He valued not just the friendship but the advice and counsel Dr. Seals felt free to give him as well. He frequently shared confidences with this friend, and some thought that probably Dr. Seals was as knowledgeable about what was going on in the church as anyone.

Another close and dear friend was I. C. Mathis. As already noted, this friend influenced Dr. Powers to make his home in Dallas, where Dr. Mathis was serving as district superintendent. However, in a particular situation that developed in a matter pertaining to I. C. Mathis, that adherence to principle prevailed over the influence of a friend. It had to do with the division of Dr. Mathis's district. The new district to be formed would become the Houston District.

Dr. Mathis had selected a man he felt should be superintendent of the new area. He shared the name with Dr. Powers. Because the new superintendent's office would be an appointed position, Dr. Mathis urged Dr. Powers to appoint Mathis's choice for the assignment. Dr. Powers was cautious in his response, simply saying he would consider it in praying about the matter.

As the time approached for the announcement to be made, Dr. Mathis brought more pressure to bear upon the general superintendent, who merely responded by saying he was still praying about it. When he actually made the appointment he did not choose the one selected by his friend but another. It proved to be a wise decision, and subsequent leadings in the life of the one he appointed, V. H. Lewis, bore this out. But it did put a strain on the friendship, a price Dr. Powers was willing to pay in order to be true to his own conscience and to what he ascertained to be the leadings of the Lord.

This commitment to basic principles for guidance in times of crisis was to be put to the test in a rather critical and sensitive matter toward the end of his tenure of service as general superintendent. It had to do with the opening of the mission work in Papua New Guinea and his son, Dr. Dudley Powers. After the initial opening of the work there and with the appointment of his own son to be in charge of the medical ministries, it was suggested he relinquish jurisdiction of the field to another general superintendent. Another decision relating to the medical work would find some disappointment in the heart of Dr. Powers. His board reduced the goal for the special offering to be raised for New Guinea from $400,000 to what they felt to be a more realistic $200,000 goal. Although both of these decisions would be questioned in his own mind, he would not let personal and family attachments prevail over united board decisions. He went along with both of them.

When Dudley and his family arrived on the field they found the hospital building not finished. It would be 18 months before it would be completed.

Subsequent changes in mission policy have separated institutional missionary councils from those related primarily to church growth. This had not as yet taken place, and differences of opinion on placement of personnel by nonmedical missionaries over and against the desires of medical missionaries resulted in tensions among the mission staff. This, along with an increasing demand on the hours of the medical personnel, began to take its toll on the physical and emotional well-being of the missionaries themselves. After 3½ years Dudley felt this assignment was completed. The hospital was now built, and the concept of medical missions was firmly established and accepted in the Highlands. The strain had resulted in other resignations, however, as well, as the field seemed to be in crisis.

The test to Dr. Powers, the father as well as the general superintedent, was found in the necessity to accept decisions which resulted in an initial funding of only one-half what he felt was necessary. In his mind at least, these additional funds would have averted the subsequent results. Furthermore, by principle he would accept decisions made between his son and other church leaders without mediation or interference on his part. He hoped, of course, that this would all pass over without permanent damage to any of the missionaries involved or the field itself.

At the last General Assembly Dr. Powers ever attended and the one in which he last participated, this time as a retiring general superintendent, the issue was brought to the floor. It was a time of suspense and not without felt tensions as Dr. Powers' own son-in-law, a General Assembly delegate, debated the matter with intense emotion. His position was one of concern on behalf of medical missionaries not just in New Guinea but elsewhere as well. Of course, his statements were directed to the situation involving his brother-in-law, Dudley Powers.

During this time of drama the eyes of the General Assembly delegates began to focus on Dr. Hardy Powers. He requested personal privilege, which was granted, and went to the microphone.

His words were clearly weighed. He knew that many delegates were aware of his personal concerns, even his disappointments. However, emotional expressions for his own family did not surface. Instead he pointed out the newness of the field, the difficulties of establishing a work of that magnitude, and that in a real sense many became the victims of pioneering a project where there was no recorded precedent on how it might be done.

Everyone came out winners. Son Dudley is held in high esteem in the church to this day and is a member of the denomination's General Board. Son-in-law Selden Kelly, by his debate, helped sharpen the conscience of the church on overworked missionaries and understaffed missions. He is a strong Nazarene layman and, along with his wife, Nona, Dr. Powers' oldest daughter, is in much demand throughout the church as a speaker in lay retreats. And Dr. Powers, true to his principled convictions, refused to compromise in any way his loyalty to the church he loved and its leadership. That day he stood very tall in the eyes of those present. It was in a sense his valedictory.

In 1958 the denomination celebrated its 50th anniversary. Dr. Powers was requested to deliver the anniversary sermon at a gathering which convened on the site in Pilot Point, Tex., where the merger took place in 1908. It was a great reunion of Nazarenes, and Dr. Powers rose to the occasion with an eloquent and dynamic presentation. His message is in itself a landmark.

The message which brought the Church [of the Nazarene] into existence included all the generally accepted doctrines of evangelical Christianity with a special emphasis on the doctrine of entire sanctification as a second work of grace, the heritage of all believers. The landmarks which have guided us in our journey for these 50 years may be like unto a mountain range. . . . Great pilot points to which they looked then and to which we look today . . .

First, the authority of Scripture. . . . To them the final arbiter of all manners of faith and practice was "What saith the Lord?" . . . Second, the adequacy of the Atonement. . . . Their ideal Christian experience was sins forgiven, the nature sanctified as a second work of grace subsequent to regeneration, and a holy, victorious life in this present world. . . . Third, the reality of Christian experience. . . . Theirs was a soul-satisfying, personal relationship to a divine personality. . . . *It is time now to take our bearings once again by gazing at those great mountain peaks of TRUTH and PRINCIPLE which guided our founding fathers.* They never change. They must never become unfamiliar to the people called Nazarenes *(capitalization and italics added)*.

Mountain peaks of *truth* and *principle* were not just scaled by the founding fathers. They were also reached and explored by this one who found himself at the helm of leadership at this important and crucial mid-centennial period in the church's history. He proved to us that the original *truths* and *principles* which guided the founding fathers continued to be valid for the church of his day. One can only assume the same would be said for the present generation of his church.

8

Human Being

As the new hospital in Papua New Guinea neared completion, there was unanimous agreement on the Board of General Superintendents that Dr. Powers should be the one to dedicate it. This was a welcome assignment, for the surrendering of this rather favorite field in jurisdictional responsibilities had been done with some reluctance. Because his son Dudley had been assigned to this mission station as resident doctor, he had, of course, maintained special interest in the work there. This would be one of his last major overseas assignments as general superintendent. Other duties were given him to cover on the same trip which would include several stopovers. It was agreed that Mrs. Powers should accompany him.

That there was concern for his health was no secret. He ordinarily had a shuffle in his walk which had uniquely characterized him. At the time of his election as general superintendent one of his friends teased him good-naturedly by suggesting he had been practicing this shuffle as preparation for his elected position. There was something different about him. This was true of his walk. There was a charisma about him that caused people to take notice when he entered a room. He had a regal bearing in his stature.

But now the shuffle was slower. There was a stoop to his shoulders, and his preaching especially seemed to be affected by failing health. His sermons lengthened considerably, as did assembly sessions over which he was presiding.

He and Mrs. Powers traveled to New Guinea. The day of dedication was a happy occasion. However, while there he became painfully aware of the unhappy situation which had developed on the field. This was the problem which eventually made its way to the floor of the General Assembly the next year. He felt the pressures of this problem very keenly. In a communique back to the home office he stated that the New Guinea assignment had been very difficult. On the way to New Guinea he and Mrs. Powers had visited the work in Samoa and New Zealand. They stopped in Australia and conducted a district assembly there. On their way home the plane landed in Singapore. En route Dr. Powers had developed chest pains, and Mrs. Powers became greatly concerned. In Singapore she requested medical help for her husband. He was taken immediately from the plane to one of Singapore's hospitals where doctors diagnosed his condition as a coronary attack.

Here Mrs. Powers found herself with a very sick husband not only in a foreign country but in one in which there was no Church of the Nazarene. She knew no one in Singapore. They were at the mercy of doctors and other hospital personnel who were total strangers to them. Understandably, it was a very difficult and trying experience for both of them.

Mrs. Powers notified international headquarters in Kansas City of the situation. Word was sent out to the church with an accompanying request for prayer for the general superintendent's recovery. After her husband had been in the Singapore hospital for a week, Mrs. Powers sent the following telegram to Kansas City over her husband's signature:

New Guinea assignment very heavy. I suffered coronary. Doctors here adamant about 30-day hospitalization. Three weeks remain. Necessary I miss first two assemblies, then able to continue. Notify board. Welcome advice. Notify children.

One cannot but appreciate the pressures this situation brought to bear on Mrs. Powers. Frequently she had traveled with her husband and was always a great source of comfort and joy to him. Now on this occasion she would have a ministry to perform which would be uniquely hers. She rose to the challenge, meeting all the bureaucratic demands of facing illness and hospitalization in a foreign country. Her family would insist their mother deserves recognition in her own right, not just for the manner in which she met this particular crisis, but for the kind of mother and wife she demonstrated herself to be throughout life. She is indeed a lovely, godly woman and is held in high esteem by those who know her.

Once back in the United States and after having sufficiently recovered from his illness, Dr. Powers assumed his duties again, determined to carry his share of the load right up to the time of his retirement at the General Assembly in 1968. He stepped into a round of district assemblies as his usual vigorous self.

District assemblies conducted by General Superintendent Powers were more likely than not happy, joyful occasions. Looking back, his life was filled with memorable experiences presiding over them.

For example, there was the session being held in a non-air-conditioned church building. It was a hot, humid summer day. Frequently during the day he had reached into his pocket for a handkerchief to wipe perspiration from his forehead. Upon arriving back in his hotel room, he pulled the handkerchief out once again. To his surprise and sudden embarrassment he found that what he thought was a handkerchief was instead a slip belonging to one of his twin daughters which had apparently been inadvertently packed in his suitcase among his handkerchiefs. He wondered how many people in the assembly session that day had perhaps observed what he had not noticed—that he was removing perspiration not with a handkerchief as he thought but with girls' lingerie instead.

Another public handkerchief episode was experienced by Dr. Powers when he was preaching on the subject of "materialism." His eldest daughter, Nona, had borrowed one of her father's handkerchiefs which she in turn had held over a light bulb, burning a large hole in it. Trying to cover up what she had done, she had seen to it that it was properly laundered and placed with the rest of his handkerchiefs.

This was the handkerchief he had in his pocket when he was preaching on "the love of money." He was endeavoring to explain how some people even will hide behind a $5.00 bill. To illustrate his point he pulled his handkerchief out, unfolded it, and held it up before his face. The large hole allowed his mouth and nose to be plainly seen, while the point of the message was clearly lost.

Then there was the time he was preaching in a camp meeting in Nashville. In one particular service he felt he was having a most difficult time delivering his sermon. A lady who was present recognized the struggle he was having but wanted to encourage him nevertheless. Her comment would hardly be interpreted as a compliment, but neither could it be considered otherwise. She said, "My, but you were certainly topping tall timber tonight."

Not willing to consider her remarks an undeserved commendation, Dr. Powers replied, "Lady, I've been in the brush many times before, but this is the first time I have ever found it that high in a tree."

Back when he was district superintendent in Iowa one of Dr. Powers' sons accompanied his father on a visit to the church in Fort Dodge. He recalls that a young student preacher was supplying the pulpit. When Dr. Powers showed up he wanted to defer to his special guest. The district superintendent, however, insisted that the young man go ahead and preach. At best it was a difficult task for the student preacher. Afterward he commented to the district superintendent, "That's the first time I've ever been in the brush in all my life."

Dr. Powers had a reassuring reply. "Young man," he said, "I've been through most all the brush there is, and I can assure you there is nothing there that will hurt you."

There was another interesting experience with a young minister in 1946. Dr. Powers was only two years into his service as a general superintendent and was on his was to an assignment in Alaska. His son Dudley was with him. They drove from Dallas to Seattle. From there they would fly on to Anchorage.

En route to Seattle they stopped in a small desert town in Arizona on Saturday evening. Finding a Nazarene church there, they planned to attend the service on Sunday morning. They arrived at the church just in time for the Sunday School "closing exercises."

The young pastor had just graduated from Bethany Nazarene College. This was his first charge as a minister. The church, a small building, was full with about 50 people present. The service began, but the preacher kept looking back at the visiting father and son. There was something familiar about the older of the two especially, but he didn't know just what. As they left the church, Dr. Powers commended the young man on the service and then said, "My name is Powers." As they drove away,

Dudley couldn't refrain from teasing his father with, "Dad, if you ever get to thinking you really are someone, I'll remind you of today."

Upon arriving in Seattle Dr. Powers received a telephone call from the Arizona district superintendent. "I have a young pastor on my district who is simply devastated," he said. In some literature which had arrived from the Nazarene Publishing House that week he had seen a picture of General Superintendent Powers. The pastor had recognized the face as that of his guest in church the previous Sunday. It was a little bit too much for the young minister when he began to remember the previous Sunday and that he had preached to a general superintendent. It was even more of a concern to him when he recalled that he hadn't even recognized Dr. Powers, let alone acknowledged his presence publicly.

The human side of Dr. Powers has left his family especially with pleasant memories. One of his boys has spoken of the first time it seemed to dawn on him that his father was human and not some sort of a super-natural being who never did any wrong. It was when he was going through some personal things of his parents and came across a picture of his father when he was a young boy. In the picture he saw his father had a cigarette in his hand. He had always thought of his father as perfect and couldn't imagine him as ever having been like others who would do things contrary to what he later believed and practiced. The son said it was a good experience for him to see that this father, like everyone else, at some time needed to experience the life-changing and habit-breaking grace of God.

What his children also learned about their father was that after he was in the ministry he sensed the Holy Spirit speaking to him of a matter which had taken place years before back in Texas. In a place where he had been working he had helped himself to some of the money in the till. He had never been caught and had forgotten about it until the Holy Spirit convicted him of it when pastoring the church in Cucamonga, Calif. He promptly responded to the conviction he received in the matter and wrote a letter to the former employer, enclosing the amount he had coming to him.

One of Dr. Powers' daughters vividly recalled being what she felt was unduly punished by her father. It had to do with something she told him, and he doubted the truth of her statement. Later that night Mrs. Powers informed her husband that his daughter had indeed related the situation as it truly was. His sensitive feelings caused him to go into the little girl's bedroom, awaken her, and ask her for forgiveness.

In the hospital, just weeks before he passed away, all three girls were visiting him. He was very weak and could hardly speak. Leaning over, the girls heard him say that he had just one major regret, and that was that he had not more perfectly exemplified the Christ he loved. To all three he said, "If I have ever done anything to disappoint you, I want you to forgive me."

One of his children has remembered her father as the master of encouragement. She often saw him demonstrate an ability to take brokenness in someone's life and make it a possibility. From shattered dreams hope would be produced. With Christ nothing was really impossible. His patient, indirect approach to dealing with the most difficult of situations has left a memorable impression on all five of his children.

His love for the church he served lingered with him to the last. To his son he said, "If anyone has something bad to say about the church, I don't want to hear it."

He struggled over the divorce issue, seeking for some divine direction which he might in turn share with his church. He knew it was to be debated at the General Assembly in 1972, and he wanted very much to be there. He was now general superintendent emeritus, and perhaps his present senior position would give him a voice of authority to help find a redemptive solution to the whole problem of divorce in our society. He secured the assistance of his oldest daughter to research the matter for him. He requested she check out the holiness classics to see what the authors of those books might have to say on the issue. After all, it was in reading a holiness classic that his father had met a spiritual crisis; and likewise, he had received spiritual victory which proved to be pivotal in his own life after reading one of the classics. Perhaps these great books would shed some light to guide his church through this time of decision.

Nona, his daughter, knowing how much her father wanted to be present at the 1972 General Assembly, prayed earnestly for her father's healing. While flying to Oklahoma City where her father was hospitalized, she read from her Bible. Her eyes fell on Heb. 12:22-23. "But ye are come unto mount Sion, and unto the city of the living God, the heavenly Jerusalem, and to an innumerable company of angels, to the general assembly and church of the firstborn, which are written in heaven, and to God the Judge of all, and to the spirits of just men made perfect."

In Bethany, just outside Oklahoma City, Nona approached the hospital room. Inside was her father who was suffering from a disease called myelofibrosis. This has to do with the drying up of the bone marrow. In the last few months he had received a total of 60 units of blood.

Outside the door to her father's room stood Dr. and Mrs. G. B. Williamson. Four times in the last two months of Dr. Powers' life this very great friend had made a special trip to be by his colleague's side in the hospital. Hardy, Jr., had recalled especially one of the previous visits when he was in the room when Dr. Williamson came in. His dad looked up at him and said, "Listen carefully, son, to what this man has to say."

Hardy, Jr., watched these two "giants of the church" who, though disagreeing frequently, had loved one another deeply. These fellow servants of their Lord firmly clasped their hands together and, as they had done so many times, prayed with each other and fervently interceded for each other.

Now it was Nona who stood facing Dr. Williamson. She shared her scripture, which to her was God's way of saying that her father would not make it to the General Assembly in Miami, Fla. Rather, he would be present at the "general assembly and church of the firstborn" in God's eternal presence.

Dr. Williamson replied that he fully understood, for in his devotions that very morning he felt God had revealed the same thing to him. Inside, Nona, Mrs. Powers, and Dr. and Mrs. Williamson stood by the side of Dr. Powers' bed. Mrs. Williamson quoted scripture as only she is able to do. Dr. Williamson prayed. Dr. Powers was so weak he could hardly express himself. But again the depth of appreciation these two men had for each other was apparent. The evidence was convincing and conclusive. It was just as Hardy Powers had always taught his family: "Pure hearts make it possible to disagree agreeably." Not only did he and his friend share this same philosophy, but both of them had proven it, and it had indeed worked.

The General Assembly in Miami began Sunday, June 18, 1972. Dr. Powers passed away June 10 at 11:17 in the morning. His funeral was held in First Church of the Nazarene in Bethany, Okla., on Tuesday, the 13th. The preliminary General Conventions were to begin the next day. Dr. Williamson and Nona both had correctly interpreted the word of the Lord.

There was no question in the minds of family members as to who should deliver the funeral address. Indeed, Dr. Powers himself had expressed his preference before passing away. The man who came within 50 votes of being chosen himself in 1944 only to be outdistanced at the time by Hardy Powers had demonstrated the sincerity of his sentiments at the time when he said the church needed Hardy Powers in 1944 in the hour of crisis. His own election as a general superintendent two years later had placed two strong men on the same board. Their ultimate aims were the same. Their methods for seeing those aims reached were often different. Now they could both look back on lives of effective leadership, and at the same time they had enjoyed an enduring friendship. The significance of G. B. Williamson's preaching the funeral sermon would find difficulty being expressed in mere words alone.

Among his private papers these words penned by Hardy Powers himself were found. No more fitting or beautiful personal testimony could summarize the life and commitment of this great man:

> Kept for Jesus and His glory
>   I would every moment be,
> Kept by Jesus through His power
>   Freely flowing unto me.
>
> Kept from sin and needless sighing,
>   Kept from fear and doubt and pride,
> Kept through trials, sharp and many,
>   Kept by Jesus crucified.

Kept mid all the world's allurements,
  Kept when passions strongly plead,
Kept mid storm and persecution,
  Kept in every time of need.

Kept for Him to do or suffer
  As His blessed will may be.
Kept for Jesus, Jesus only.
  Kept through all eternity.

Appendix A

This is a digest of the message given at funeral services for General Superintendent Emeritus Hardy C. Powers, Bethany, Okla., June 13, 1972, by G. B. Williamson, general superintendent emeritus.

"They that be wise shall shine as the brightness of the firmament; and they that turn many to righteousness as the stars for ever and ever" (Dan. 12:3).

Since learning of the serious impairment of Dr. Powers' health several months ago, these words by Daniel have been in my mind as related to him, literally hundreds of times. They have a special fitness for our loved one, friend, colleague, and fellow worker for Christ.

General Superintendent Powers was a wise man. His was the wisdom that is from above, "pure, then peaceable, gentle, and easy to be entreated, full of mercy and good fruits" (James 3:17). To this friend of God and man the fear of the Lord was the beginning of wisdom.

Hardy C. Powers showed himself to be wise in his early choices. As a young banker, he selected Ruby Mae King to be his companion of more than 50 good and happy years. The thousands who have known the Powers family will testify that his choice was a wise one. She has been the strong anchor for her husband and family—a virtuous woman whose price is far above rubies. Her own works praise her.

Dr. Powers proved his wisdom as a family man. Duties took him from home on long journeys often, but he was always the patriarch and high priest of his own household. His exemplary life, wise counsel, and constant prayers have been rewarded in the remarkable family of five children and 17 grandchildren who do him honor today.

The wisest of all his choices was made when he, like Moses, took a clear look at the alternatives and chose eternal values because he endured as seeing Him who is invisible.

As a wise man, he chose the locale of his early ministry. Viewing the record from this vantage point, it is the shining path of a man of destiny. To use his words, he began as pastor of the First Church of the Nazarene of Cucamunga (sic), Calif. There God was pleased to bless his labors. It was there on a Monday afternoon he had a lone confrontation with God. It was his Peniel. Like Jacob, he refused to leave the place until God met him in sanctifying grace. At about four o'clock the Holy Spirit came to cleanse, to fill, and to abide forever.

Dr. J. W. Short observed the promising pastor and youth leader. Soon the elder admirer moved to Iowa to become district superintendent. When one of his key churches was without a pastor, the promising, youthful Hardy Powers was called to fill the vacancy. It was to be a prosperous ministry. The church grew in strength and deepened in spirituality. In seven years 17 persons responded to God's call to full-time Christian service. For a number of years the pastor was the district president of the NYPS.

Hardy Powers was elected district superintendent at the age of 36. During his eight years in that office the Iowa District enjoyed unprecedented development. The name of Dr. Hardy C. Powers came to be known across the church as a gifted soul winner and a wise leader.

In the General Assembly of 1944, God and His people looked for "a man" to "stand in the gap" (Ezek. 22:30). He found one in the person of Hardy C. Powers, who by choice of the delegation and in the wise providence of God was to assume the heavy burdens of the general superintendency.

It was in times that tried men's souls. Dr. Powers was to be the man to link the leadership of the past to the swiftly changing present and the onrushing future. As God's mysterious will determined, this new leader was to serve with Roy T. Williams for the last 2 of his 30 years in office, with James B. Chapman for the last of his 19 years, and with Howard V. Miller for the last 4½ of his 8½ years.

It soon was evident that the new leader had the confidence of his colleagues and of the entire church. He had the bearing of one who walked with kings and had the common touch. He possessed the grace, the stability, the sense of direction, and the firm patience to draw men together for fellowship and service in building the Church of Jesus Christ.

He saw clearly that God's people wanted and needed the guidance that a Board of General Superintendents molding variety into unity could provide. To such a purpose and policy Dr. Powers dedicated all the 24 years he served as a leader, trusted and beloved. During that time the Church of the Nazarene more than doubled in membership and carried its message of scriptural holiness to many new world areas.

Because he was wise, General Superintendent Powers will shine on with the brightness of the firmament. No historian of the Church of the Nazarene can deny to him a permanent place in the record of that quarter of a century to which he in a special sense belonged.

The second portion of Daniel's words adds a further description of the man to whom we pay our tribute of love today. It also includes a quality of the reward that he now enjoys—"They that turn many to righteousness [shall shine] as the stars for ever and ever."

The crowning glory of the wisdom of our loved one, friend, and fellow laborer was his skill as a soul winner. The wise man of long ago said, "He that winneth souls is wise" (Prov. 11:30). As pastor, district superintendent, general superintendent, and general superintendent emeritus, he was an evangelistic preacher. Soul winning was his master passion. He saw long altars lined with earnest seekers. There was always a note of reality in his message. He was never impersonal or professional. He was faithful in bearing his witness to individuals among those with whom he did business and among those he met in casual acquaintaince.

On airplanes he drew fellow passengers into conversation and confession of spiritual need. On more than one occasion he prayed with them and led them to the Savior.

When Dr. Powers was a patient in the hospital during the long months of his last illness, one of his doctors acknowledged that life did not have the meaning and satisfaction he longed for. Dr. Powers said, "Yours is a need deep within you." Not long after, about 2 A.M., there was a gentle tapping on his door. Responding to the invitation to enter, the doctor and his wife came in. The patient led the doctor to the healing experience of saving grace.

His last pastoral call was on a fellow patient whose heart hunger he knew. He arose from his bed, put on slippers and a robe, and walked down the hall to pray with the person who had confided in him.

When the saints come marching home, among them will be the many who have turned to righteousness through the influence and loving ministry of Hardy C. Powers. They shall come from across this continent and from Europe, Africa, Asia, South America, Australia, and the islands of the sea to sit down with Abraham, Isaac, and Jacob in the eternal kingdom of the Father. They will see the Savior, who loved them and washed them from their sins in Hiw own precious blood. They will also see the man who told them the story of Jesus and His great salvation. They will find him shining as the stars for ever and ever.

Appendix B

This poem was composed by Hardy C. Powers on December 3, 1952, just after he had bidden farewell to African missionaries at the airport in Johannesburg, South Africa. He and his wife boarded the BOAC Comet jetliner. Then, climbing toward the stratosphere on the way to New York, he wrote the following:

THE MISSIONARY BAND

Some seek for pleasure
Under skies of blue azure
  On lazy lagoons by the seas.
Other have a yen
For the high mountain glen,
  Or a cruise in a tropical breeze.

But I know a band
Who hail from all lands,
  Who are attracted by none of these things.
They've heard a call from a Cross
And count all else but loss,
  To the lost the glad tidings to bring.

I've met them far north
and in the deep south,
  And abroad from the east to the west.
And the reason they're there
Is neither scenery nor air
  But sin's pain deep in man's breast.

They're the missionary band,
And their spirit is grand,
  Untouched by the selfish or base.
When heaven's gate swings wide,
I expect to see them inside
  With the sheaves they have won by His grace.

Appendix C

The following is a letter shared by the eldest son of Hardy Powers, which he received from his father to motivate him in full payment of budgets in his local church. Although a personal letter, it is extremely significant for all pastors, especially in the Church of the Nazarene.

Dear Hardy:

Enclosed please find check for $100 to be applied on budgets *only*—not for local operating expense. If your treasurer feels he cannot apply it on budgets, please return it to me immediately. I do not wish to give it for any other purpose. I would like to be one of five men who would give at least $100 each on budgets. If you can use it as a lever to raise the *balance* on budgets I would be glad.

I am a great believer in budgets. I saw a man saved in Alaska who is now a big international businessman pouring thousands of dollars back into the work—because of budgets.

I saw the manager of Honolulu's largest radio station pray through—he testified to me about a month ago—still saved—all because of budgets.

I saw an African witch doctor weep his way through to Christ and victory—we gathered around a bonfire in the yard while he burned his "medicine" and sang the praises of God—because someone paid the budget.

I saw about 300 people seeking God in one service in Africa—the budgets made it possible.

I saw a veteran missionary who had given her *life* in unselfish services for others—stricken ill but hospitalized and cared for by the church because someone was unselfish and paid the budget.

The woman of Zarephath gave her last cake to the cause of God and thereby found the solution to her personal problems.

A small home mission church was organized, and they conducted a revival—I was saved—because someone cared enough to pay the budget.

Christ gave His all on the Cross—the birds had nests, the foxes had holes, but He had no place to lay His head—it was all for me. And if I have not the spirit of Christ toward others—I am none of His.

The widow gave two mites—all her living—and became immortal by so doing. Her deed was measured not so much by the amount she gave but by what she had left. Christ was so concerned He was watching that offering that day. And He still takes note when we raise the budget today. For when we plead for this, Christ pleads, because the budget is the only chance that soul in Africa, India, New Guinea will have to find Christ. He can't plead for himself, so someone here must speak for him.

We are praying,
Much love,
Dad

Appendix D

This essay titled "How to Manage Grandpa!" was found among the private papers of Dr. Powers. It speaks both of his warm affection for family as well as his real-life situation applications to spiritual living.

He's only three, towheaded, and with a twinkle in his eye. But he has instinctively discovered a secret which his elders sometimes overlook. It is the ingenuity and resourcefulness of love.

He has never attended a "how convention." It would be impossible for him to articulate the mechanics of "Managing His Grandpa." His vocabulary is very limited. His approach is varied. But he always communicates one thing, and that is his love. It shines through his bright, blue eyes, his sometimes awkward movements, and his stumbling speech. But it is always there.

It also has some side effects. It makes Grandpa putty in his hands. It secures for him unsolicited ice-cream cones, a place in the front seat of the family car, and an unscheduled interruption in Grandpa's reading program for a romp on the floor.

But all these things are secondary. His love is primary. He is only three, but he seems to know that "love never faileth." It shines through all his unconscious actions and motivates all he does. You wouldn't believe the ingenuity he demonstrates from time to time.

If I am not mistaken it would be a great disappointment to Grandpa if this "wee lad" should become totally obsessed with the "how" of his techniques and actions and lose sight of the "why" those techniques are successful. Perfected techniques—important though they are—

are not almighty. They must be prompted by love. Love is the indispensable ingredient.

Perhaps those of us who are older could learn a lesson from this little towhead. Maybe it was what the Master had in mind when He asked Peter the question, "Lovest thou me?" This question no doubt was designed to focus attention on the heart condition of His disciple which was the source of his motivation. The Lord then called attention to his task—that of feeding His sheep. Three times He asked the question, and three times He gave the command to carry out the task of feeding the sheep. So we see there is a most vital connection between our heart condition and the success or failure of our task. The "how" we feed the sheep is important, but the "why" we feed them is all-important.

Grandpa thinks so too.